LETTERS TO A N(

Thomas Crean O.P.

Letters to a Non-Believer

GRACEWING

Originally published in 2009
by Family Publications

This edition 2012

Gracewing
2 Southern Avenue
Leominster
Herefordshire HR6 0QF

www.gracewing.co.uk

The right of Thomas Crean, OP to be identified as the author
of this work has been asserted in accordance with the
Copyright, Designs and Patents Act 1988.

ISBN 978 0 85244 762 8

To Our Lady of Fatima

Contents

Preface 11

Letter 1 – On the existence of God 12

Letter 2 – On the nature of God 17

Letter 3 – On the Holy Trinity 23

Letter 4 – On faith 28

Letter 5 – On the trustworthiness of the Gospels 33

Letter 6 – On Jesus Christ 38

Letter 7 – On the Incarnation 43

Letter 8 – On the Resurrection 48

Letter 9 – On Christ's death 54

Letter 10 – On Christ's death *(cont'd.)* 58

Letter 11 – On the Fall of Man 63

Letter 12 – On science and the Fall of Man 68

Letter 13 – On the love of God 74

Letter 14 – On love for our enemies 79

Letter 15 – On the soul 84

Letter 16 – On life after death 90

Letter 17 – On free will 95

Letter 18 – On evil and suffering 102

Letter 19 – On the need for the Church 108

Letter 20 – On recognizing the true Church 114

Letter 21 – On the Pope 121

Letter 22 – On the unchangeableness of the faith.... 127

Letter 23 – On an objection to the last letter 132

Letter 24 – On the Sacraments.......................... 137

Letter 25 – On holy baptism 142

Letter 26 – On fasting and forbidden foods 147

Letter 27 – On those outside the Church............. 152

Letter 28 – On those outside the Church *(cont'd.)*.... 156

Letter 29 – On prayer.................................... 161

Letter 30 – On eternity.................................. 166

Letter 31 – On marriage 171

Letter 32 – On fruitfulness in marriage................ 177

Letter 33 – On following Christ........................ 182

Preface

St Peter told his spiritual children to be ready to satisfy those who might seek a reason for their hope. The present work is a modest attempt to do just that. The letters are addressed not to a hostile non-believer, who desires Christianity to be false, nor to a careless non-believer who assumes that it is, but to a honest enquirer, who wants 'to follow the argument wherever it leads'.

It may be asked why the recipient of these letters is a Muslim, or at least has an Islamic name. A letter must be addressed to someone, and many people in our society bear Islamic names. If any of them should ever see this book, I hope that they will be pleased that the letter writer has considered some questions or objections that Muslims have before now put to Catholics. But the work as a whole is not offered to Muslims only. It is offered to anyone who is looking for truth amid the conflicting opinions of the world, and who does not despair of finding it.

Thomas Crean O.P.

Feast of St Bonaventure,
A.D. 2009

Letter One

ON THE EXISTENCE OF GOD

Dear Ali,

I was happy to meet you the other day at your college and to hear that you'd like to know some more about what Catholics believe. By the way, in case you were wondering, a Catholic isn't something different from a Christian: it's a kind of Christian. In fact, Catholics consider themselves to be just the same as the first Christians. We'd say that all the other groups called 'Christian' lack something or other of what Christ came to give us. But perhaps we can discuss that later, if you're still interested.

Anyway, first things first! You told me the other day that despite having been brought up as a Muslim, when you came to university and took up the study of philosophy, you began to wonder whether God really exists at all. And you asked me whether I thought it was possible to prove that He does, beyond all doubt. I promised then that I'd put some ideas on paper and let you have them. So this is what I'm doing now.

First of all, I do believe it's possible to use our minds to show that God exists. I know that some people would say that this is presumptuous: they would say that because God is so much greater than us, we should just adore

Him, not reason about Him. But I think that's a mistake. Of course we should adore God first and foremost. But, after all, who gave us a mind if not God? And why would He have given us a mind unless He wanted us to use it? It would be presumptuous if we thought that we with our limited minds could understand God through and through; but it's not presumptuous to try to know something about Him. So it says in our Bible: 'By the greatness of the beauty of created things, the creator of them may be seen'. Not seen in the way that we see each other, of course, but known – rather as we can know there is someone with us in a dark room, even though we can't see his face.

So, since the Bible says that we should be able to know God by created things, let's try to see exactly how, in a way that should satisfy the most rigorous of philosophers. (I say that it *should* be able to satisfy them, not that it certainly *will*. When it comes to something as life-changing as the existence of God, people can have strong motives to resist even good arguments.) Take any created thing you like – yourself, for instance. Of course, we don't begin by assuming that you or anything else is *created*, as that would be begging the question of whether there is a creator or not. I just mean, consider yourself, Ali, as you are. You know that you have not always existed. You came into being some twenty-one years ago. Before that you were possible, so to speak, but not actual. Now you are actual: but you won't go on for ever. Don't get me wrong – I'm not denying that you have an immortal soul. I just mean that you, like myself and everyone else, will die one day. After that, Ali will no longer exist, only Ali's soul will exist (until the resurrection, which Catholics, like Muslims, believe in).

This shows that Ali is not a *necessary* being. There's nothing in the nature of Ali that says that he must exist, or else the world couldn't have been going for so many centuries without you. And once you do exist, there's nothing in your nature that says you must go on existing for ever. On the contrary, you and I will both die one day, and then our bodies will return to the ground – not just be put into the ground, but decay until they actually become a part of the earth.

Technically speaking, we say that you're a *contingent* being. A contingent being is something that exists, but doesn't need to exist. It doesn't exist *by its very nature*. In fact, all the things we can see and touch are contingent beings, which is why they're all due to come to an end one day. Even the stars wear out eventually, or so we're told.

So a contingent being doesn't have to exist, yet it does exist. Obviously then, it gets its existence from something outside itself, something which explains why it exists when it doesn't need to. What is this in your case? You might be thinking: 'that's easy – it's my parents. It was because of them that I came into existence twenty-one years ago.'

Of course that's true: but it's not the whole truth. It's not just that you were a contingent being twenty-one years ago. You are one *now*. At the precise moment that you read this, there is *nothing* in your nature that says that you must exist. Yet you do exist. Why is this? You might say, 'Because of the air I breathe'. Yes – but you must first exist in order to be able to breathe. Why at this moment do you exist? It's not because of your parents now: they're not even in the same country as you. They brought you into being — but what is keeping you in existence *now*?

Each of us is, so to speak, constantly suspended over an abyss of nothingness. There is something which is stopping us from falling into this abyss, by holding us in being. It's not ourselves: no one can be the cause of his own existing, because a cause is always something different from the thing it acts on. So what is it?

Perhaps someone will say that it is simply the universe itself. The particular arrangement of matter in the universe, with all the forces that result from this arrangement, explain why Ali exists now. Maybe it is so. But in that case, I'll ask another question: this arrangement of matter, this particular configuration of the forces of the universe, is it something necessary? Has it always been as it is now, and will it always be so for the future? Obviously, the answer is no. The present state of the universe is just as contingent as you are. The universe is changing all the time. There's nothing in the nature of matter to say that it must be arranged as it now is; if there were, it wouldn't be able to change.

In other words, even if we say that the arrangement of the rest of the universe is the cause of your existing now, we haven't reached the end. The arrangement of the rest of the universe is just as contingent, just as 'un-necessary' as you are yourself. So it too needs a cause: the present arrangement of the universe needs an explanation outside itself just as much as you do. What can the explanation be? Clearly, we have to come eventually to something which is not contingent: something which not only does exist but *must* exist. We must come to something which couldn't have been any different from what it is. And this is what we call 'God'. You might never have existed; the particular arrangement of the forces of the universe which helps keep you in being might never have been what it is; but God could not have not existed. If He could have failed to exist, or been different from what He is, He would not be God.

To put the argument very simply: if a contingent being exists, a necessary being exists; but a contingent being exists; therefore a necessary being exists.

I'm afraid that was all rather abstract – still, you *are* studying philosophy. Tell me what you think, and what you'd like to discuss next.

With best wishes,

Christophorus

Letter Two

ON THE NATURE OF GOD

Dear Ali,

Thanks for your speedy reply and its searching questions. I'll do my best to answer them in this letter.

First, you say you're not quite sure why the universe itself couldn't be the necessary being, or the thing that exists 'of itself' with no further cause. The simple answer is that nothing which is complex, that's to say, made up of several parts, can be a truly necessary being. Whenever we see something with more than one part, we can ask the question, 'How did those parts come together?' That's true whether it's a natural thing, like a man, or an artificial thing like a piano. They're made up of parts, and so we can ask what causes this bone to be joined to this bone, or this hammer to this string.

Now the universe is obviously made up of many different parts. Therefore it can't itself be the First Thing. There must be some reason why the various parts of the universe are related as they are. Even if you supposed, as some imaginative physicists do, that the universe was once just a very dense 'ball' of matter, that ball itself would have had parts. Every material thing has material parts. It's not completely simple. Therefore no material thing can be the First Thing, the necessary being which exists of itself. Every material being must depend on something which is perfectly simple and non-material. And this is God.

But secondly you ask, who keeps God in being? And if we say 'nothing', doesn't that mean that His existence is in a sense 'absurd', having no explanation? Here we have to distinguish between a reason and a cause. Nothing 'keeps' God in being, because He is Himself the first cause of all that is. Nor does He cause Himself to exist, because as I mentioned last time, nothing can be the cause of itself, just as nothing can be prior to itself. Yet His existence isn't absurd; it has a reason, namely His own nature. It is the very nature of God to exist. That's why when He revealed Himself to Moses in the burning bush, He said 'I am who am', and, 'I am He who is.'

Thirdly you want to know what we could say to those who argue that this universe receives its being from some other universe, and that universe from a third, and so on for ever, without us ever coming to some fully necessary being. The short answer is that a chain of causes must always include a first cause. One snooker ball can be moved by a second, a second by a third, a third by a fourth, but if there was no one using a snooker cue at the beginning, then none of the balls would be moved. Where there's no first cause, the other causes can't operate, and so nothing will happen. Even if our universe was kept in being by another universe, and that universe by a third, we'd have eventually to come to some being which needs no cause, and that is God.

By the way, I'm not trying to prove here that the universe had a *beginning*. I do believe that, as a Catholic, but this isn't the point I'm making. What I'm saying is that since there are beings, such as you and I, which don't exist of themselves, there must be something which does exist of itself, whose very nature is *to be*. This would be true even if there'd always been contingent things of some sort or another in existence.

Your next question was particularly interesting. Granted, you say, that there must be an absolutely necessary being, who's to say that this is a personal being – in other words, that it's God in the sense in which believers use the word. Or as you put it, 'How do we know that the necessary being is wise and good, and that He hears our prayers?'

I'll have to leave the subject of prayer to another time. But I'd like to explain why I think that God must be personal – even leaving on one side what He's revealed to mankind about Himself. It's a sound principle of philosophy that wherever there's a cause and an effect, the cause must be at least as 'perfect', that's to say, at least as rich in its nature as the effect. Let's take some obvious examples. If we're using a gas-stove to bring some water to boiling point, then the flame must be at least 212°F; if it was colder, it couldn't bring the water to be 212°F itself. Or take teaching: no one can teach someone a subject, say pure mathematics, unless they already know it themselves. In other words, 'You can't give what you don't have'.

Let's apply this to God. If He is the cause of all contingent beings, He must be at least as perfect as they are. But anything which is impersonal is *less perfect* than anything which is personal. Being personal means, for example, being able to know things – being able to know oneself and to know others. And that is always better than not being able to know things. A mountain is much bigger than a man, but the man, whoever he is, is superior to the mountain. He knows that it's there, but it doesn't know that he is.

That's why God must be personal. If He were impersonal He'd be less perfect than human beings; but then He couldn't be their cause.

Of course, when we say that God is personal, we don't mean that He is personal *in exactly the same way* as we human beings are. For one thing, He doesn't have a body: He is Spirit. God doesn't have a body because a body is made up of different parts, and as I said before, God can't have parts of any kind. Again, God doesn't know things as we do, by learning them. Nor does He have to deduce one thing from another. He knows all things, past, present and future, in one, eternal 'glance'.

Now for your last question. You say that if the existence of some contingent being, such as yourself, proves that there must be some necessary being, how do we know that there is only *one* necessary being? What if every contingent being were caused by a different necessary being? In other words, can we prove that there's only one God?

Of course Catholics believe that there's only one God, and I think we can prove it like this. Whenever we find something existing in a limited way, we can ask why it exists to this degree rather than another. For example, if we find heat 'existing' at 50 degrees in some water, we can ask why the heat is of this particular intensity, and the answer will have to do with the temperature of the flame beneath the water and the length of time for which the water has been on the flame. We explain this particular, limited intensity of heat with reference to something outside itself. What we don't say is that it's the very nature of heat to exist at 50 degrees. If it were, we'd never find it at 40 degrees or at 60.

Take another example. Let's say that I have a certain, limited knowledge of English history. We can ask, can't we, why I have this amount of knowledge, and not more or less? The answer will have to do with the people who've taught me and the books I've read. What we don't say is that 'knowledge of English history', wherever it's found, must exist in precisely the degree to which I happen to have it. For other people have more or less knowledge than I do.

So a limited quality has a cause outside itself. But this cause must be something which in some way has the quality that it passes on, since nothing can give what it doesn't have. The fire that heats the water is itself hot; the people who taught me history or who wrote the history books that I've read have a certain knowledge of the subject. But now: does the cause of this limited quality, whatever it is, also have this quality in a limited way? If it does, then it also requires a cause. Whatever degree of heat is in the flame beneath the water, it's not the very nature of heat to have that intensity: heat doesn't exist at that degree *of itself*; so it must exist at that degree because it's *caused* to do so by another. Whatever knowledge of history is in my teachers, it's not the very nature of knowledge to exist to that particular extent; knowledge doesn't exist to that extent *of itself*; so it must exist to that extent because it's *caused* by another. Whatever is limited, is caused.

But since we can't extend a causal chain indefinitely,

we must always arrive, as the explanation of any quality, at some First Thing which is *unlimited*. This, of course, is God.

But if God is unlimited, there can't be two gods. If there were two gods, they'd have to be different in some respect, since otherwise they'd be one, not two. But to be different, one of them must have something that the other lacks. In that case, the one that lacked something would be limited in some way. But if he was limited, he would need a cause, and so he wouldn't be the First Thing. So there can only be one God.

Did that make sense to you? Let me know if it didn't. Of course there's lots more one could say about the nature of God, but I hope I've given you enough to be going on with for now. And since it's better to hear what God says about Himself than to talk about Him ourselves, let me finish with a quotation from our scriptures:

> Though we speak much we cannot reach the end, and the sum of our words is 'He is all'.
>
> Where shall we find strength to praise Him? For He is greater than all His works.
>
> For the Lord has made all things, and to the godly He has granted wisdom.

With best wishes,
  Christophorus

Letter Three

ON THE HOLY TRINITY

Dear Ali,

I'm glad to hear that my letters so far have helped to allay your doubts or difficulties about God's existence. But you're puzzled by something that you've heard that Christians believe. You were told, as a boy, that we believe that God is 'three'. In that case, how can we say that there is only one God? Or how can I say, as I did in my last letter, that God has no parts, not even 'spiritual' parts?

Let me begin by repeating what I said last time, that there is and can be only one God. He Himself says, speaking through the prophet Isaiah, 'I am the Lord, that is my name; my glory I give to no other.' Many Catholics have been martyred, especially in the early years of the Church, for refusing to admit that there could be more than one God.

Still, what you've heard is correct: there is a sense in which we say that God is also three. Not that there are three gods, but that the one, true, living God is in a certain sense three. To understand what we mean by this, you'll need to think about the difference between these two words, 'person' and 'nature'.

A person is *who* someone is; a nature is *what* something is. So if someone were to ask who we are, the answer in my case would be Christophorus, in yours Ali. But if someone were to ask what we are, the answer would be the same in each case, a man. We are different persons, but we have an identical nature. Yet this same nature, though it's identical in you and me, exists twice over, so to speak, once in you and once in me.

Now the divine nature cannot exist twice, but only once – for otherwise there would be two gods, which is impossible, as I argued in my last letter. But it is possible that in this one, unrepeatable divine nature, there should be more than one Person. That wouldn't mean that there was more than one God, but simply that there was more than one divine Person, *each of whom is the one, true God.*

I say this is possible, but in fact, we couldn't be sure it was possible except by knowing that it's really true. And we can only know that it's true by knowing that God has revealed it to us.

But according to our holy scriptures, this is one of the things that God has revealed to us for our salvation: that He is three divine Persons in the one divine nature. The one God is the Father, the Word and the Holy Spirit. The Father is God, the Word is God and the Holy Spirit is God: not three different gods, but each is the one, true God.

How can this be? When we say that God is Father, you have to put out of your mind anything to do with physical fatherhood. It's not a physical fatherhood but an *intellectual* one. Think of it like this. Every human being has a certain, limited knowledge of himself. In other words, you have a *concept* of yourself, and I have one of myself. Now imagine that you knew yourself perfectly. Imagine that there was no part of your life, past, present or future, which escaped your gaze; that every chemical reaction in your body and every motive of your soul was known to you perfectly. In that case your concept of yourself would be perfect. It would be just as full and rich as you are.

Now from all eternity God knows Himself perfectly. In other words, He has a perfect 'concept' of Himself. This is what we call His *Word*. But this Word is not one of His creatures, since God didn't need to create anything in order to know who He is. God's Word must be uncreated: but this means that the Word of God must *be* God, since only God is uncreated. In other words, God's concept of Himself is not something less than Himself, as a man's concept of himself is always less than the man. The Father who conceives and the Word who is conceived are both of them personal and living. Each possesses the one divine nature. Each is the one God.

You might ask, 'All the same, why do Christians use the word "Father" when they speak of the first Person in God?' The simple answer is that Jesus Christ taught us to do so. But there's also an explanation in what I've just said. The second Person comes from the first Person and He is also His exact image. And because human sons come from their fathers and generally resemble them, the second Person is called the Son, and the first Person is called the Father.

Who then is the Holy Spirit? The Holy Spirit, also called the Spirit of God, is the third Person 'in' God. He's not a creature, not even the highest kind of creature. He is God, just as much as the Father and the Son. He is eternal and uncreated as they are. We say that He 'proceeds' from the Father and the Son, as the Son proceeds from the

Father. But how exactly are we to think about Him?

I said a moment ago that everyone has a certain knowledge of himself. It's also true that everyone has a certain love of himself. We all naturally wish ourselves well, by desiring to be happy, and this is to love ourselves. Well, God also must have a love of Himself. Of course, His love for Himself doesn't take the form of wishing Himself well, because He has every kind of perfection and happiness within Himself already. It takes the form of delighting in Himself: God is glad to be Himself. But whenever we love something, the thing that we love must exist in us, by 'shaping' our love to be *a love of that thing* and not something else. So if I love a person, then even though I may be separated from that person by many miles or several oceans, that person is already dwelling 'in' me, to the extent that he or she is 'stamping' my love, making it precisely a love of him or her, not of someone else.

Now because God loves Himself, we must say that He dwells in Himself, eternally 'drawing' His own love to Himself. And this is the Holy Spirit: the Holy Spirit is God as eternally drawing forth God's own love. This is why the Holy Spirit, like the Son, is equal to the Father; each is eternally the one, true God.

So this is what we call the mystery of the Holy Trinity. A mystery is something above reason, something that we can't fully understand in this life. Yet if we were able to see God as He is – see Him with our spirit, since He can't be seen by bodily eyes – then we should understand why God must be the Holy Trinity, and how each of the Persons, though really distinct from the other two, *is* the true God.

Do you think, all the same, that the God of the Christians is less than perfectly one – that He would be 'more' one if He were not also a Trinity of Persons? I should say just the opposite: that it's only in the mystery of the Trinity that we see how amazingly 'one' God really is. If there are three persons, each of whom is a man, there will be three men. But when there are three 'Persons', each of whom is God, there is only one God. In other words, the divine nature is so perfectly one, that it can't be multiplied, *even when it is possessed by more than one Person!*

But finally, do realize that I haven't been trying to prove the Trinity to you as I tried in my earlier letters to prove the existence of God. It's not something we can prove, because it's about God's own inner life. It's something that we can only know because God has revealed it, and which we have to accept on faith. As St John the Apostle says, 'If we accept the testimony of men [that is, of honest men], the testimony of God is greater' – for He's not only honest, He is truth itself.

With best wishes,
Christophorus

Letter Four

ON FAITH

Dear Ali,

You write, 'If I knew that God had clearly said that He was a Trinity, I should be willing to believe it; but how can I know that He has? Do I just have to take it on faith?' And you put forward this dilemma: 'If there is evidence for something, I don't need faith to believe it. If there is no evidence for something, I ought not to believe it. So there doesn't seem to be ever a reason to have faith in something.' A good objection – but I think there's an answer.

Let's think what we mean by *evidence*. I'd say that there are two main kinds of evidence, which I'll call 'direct' and 'indirect'. Direct evidence is what we have when we can see for ourselves that something is true. I can look out of my window and see that the sun is shining. What I see is sufficient evidence for me to be able to say with perfect confidence, 'The sun is shining'. There's no room for faith here, I agree.

But what about this sentence, 'The sun is shining in Australia'? I don't have any direct evidence about whether this is true or false. But I can still make a judgment about it. How? *By consulting someone who does have direct evidence.* I can watch a global weather report on the television, or I can ring a friend who lives in Australia. In either case I'll be in contact with someone who has direct evidence, and provided that there's no reason for me to doubt what they say, I'll believe their report. In that way I can know what the weather is over there, without any direct evidence, but by a kind of faith, a faith in human beings.

There can even be a chain of witnesses. I could find out the weather in Australia not by calling my friend who lives there, but by calling someone who has just been speaking to my friend. That way I'll be one more step removed from the direct evidence, but provided that both people are trustworthy, there will be no rational ground for me to doubt what I learn by means of this chain. I'll learn the truth by a *human faith* in these two people.

Now when Catholics speak about faith they mean that the one who has the direct evidence is God Himself. God knows, for example, that He is a Trinity. What's more, God is entirely trustworthy: more so than even the best of human beings. So when God reveals something to us, even though we have no direct evidence for it, we're wise to believe it. We should be acting irrationally if we didn't believe it, just as if we disbelieved a trustworthy friend in Australia who told us that it was a sunny day.

This is called *divine faith*: believing that something is true because God has said it. We say this is very important: in fact, it's one of the three qualities we need if we're to go to heaven (the others are hope and charity). Imagine that you are trapped underground in a mine-shaft, and someone lowers a rope for you to tie around your waist. Well, coming to faith is like tying on that rope. The rope doesn't bring you out of the hole straightaway, but it does enable you to be gradually hauled to safety. So if we have faith that what God says is true, we can learn what we need to do, and so gradually be lifted up by Him to eternal life. (By the way, just as the rope comes down from above, so faith is a gift from God. He doesn't just *tell* us what is true about Himself and about us; He also gives us the power to believe it.)

But I haven't yet answered your first question. Granted, you say, that we should believe what God tells us, how can we be sure about what He has told us – or even if He has 'spoken' at all? I can learn from my friend in Australia, because when I speak to him on the phone I hear his voice, which I recognise. So do Catholics claim that they hear God speaking to them, telling them what to believe?

No, we don't say that. We say that God has *already* spoken, once for all, long before anyone now living was born. But we don't say that people must believe this just because we say so; we invite them to look at the evidence from history.

Just consider, first of all, the spread of Christianity. Jesus Christ was put to death about the year AD 33, and His followers began preaching the news of His Resurrection almost immediately. They preached principally in the Roman Empire, and the Empire responded by outlawing the faith. For nearly three hundred years they were persecuted by the Empire in the most savage ways. We have a book called the 'Martyrology' which gives some accounts for every day of the year of how people died for their faith in Christ. Opening it at random, I find this:

The 25th day of August: at Rome, the holy martyrs Eusebius, Pontian, Vincent and Peregrinus. Under the Emperor Commodus, they were first placed on the rack and stretched with ropes. Then they were beaten with clubs and their sides burnt with fire. Since they faithfully continued to the end to praise Christ, they were beaten with leaden-tipped whips until they died.

That is just one. There were countless thousands of such martyrs in the Empire. Yet even though the Emperors were persecuting the Church so violently, *they couldn't stop it from spreading*. Why not? The early Christian writers report that God worked miracles through members of the Church, miracles which were so great and well-known that they convinced vast numbers to become Christians. But let's say that they were mistaken, and that no miracles were seen. Wouldn't it then be the greatest miracle of all that so many were ready not just to die, but to die joyfully in torments with faith in Christ?

Other religions have their martyrs as well, you may say. True: if people are very attached to a religion, they may be willing to die rather than give it up, just as people may be ready to die rather than to betray their family or their country. But where else does one hear of a religion that *grows from nothing by martyrdom*, with no official support from any government, and with no power to defend itself by material weapons? Remember that these martyrs weren't at war with the Empire: they wanted to be loyal citizens. The Church didn't allow them to fight the people who were persecuting them, nor to plot against the authorities. The Church always told its members to obey the Emperor in all things, unless he commanded a sin, and then to refuse, but peacefully. How then did the twelve apostles whom Christ left behind Him finish by converting this vast and hostile Empire? Could they have done it at all, unless God had been with them?

That is the kind of thing I mean, my friend, when I say that one should look at the evidence from history to see where God has spoken. And miracles, by the way, didn't come to an end after the first few centuries of Christianity. You can always find them somewhere in the Catholic Church. Not that they are ever *common*. If they were, they wouldn't make the same impression on us, and so they'd lose their point. God wants miracles to be rare, so as to be striking. But He never leaves His Church entirely without them.

However, I shouldn't want you to think that our faith depends on these miracles that God continues to work down the ages. Our faith begins with what history tells us about the life of Christ. But I'll have to leave that now to my next letter.

With best wishes,
Christophorus

Letter Five

ON THE TRUSTWORTHINESS OF THE GOSPELS

Dear Ali,

You say that you're looking forward to reading what I say about Jesus Christ, but first you want to know how we can be sure of the truth about Him. Is there any evidence from secular historians that He actually existed? You've heard that the Gospels weren't written till many years after Christ's life on earth, and also that there are lots of differences between the various Gospels. Finally you want to know what I think about the so-called 'apocryphal gospels' which you've seen mentioned in the newspapers – are they gospels that have been hidden away by the Church?

First of all, yes, we know from secular historians that Christ really existed. He is not a myth. The great Roman historian Tacitus, who was born in the middle of the first century, tells us that Christ suffered in Judaea whilst Pontius Pilate was Governor, under the emperor Tiberius. He's very hostile to Christians, calling them 'enemies of the human race', but he knows that their founder was someone real. The Jewish historian Josephus, who was born 20 years earlier, also mentions Him. Pliny the Younger, writing around AD 110, says that Christians meet on Sundays in His honour, just as we do today.

But of course our main source of knowledge about Christ is the gospel. There are four Gospels, written by St Matthew, St Mark, St Luke and St John. Two of these men, St Matthew and St John belonged to Christ's twelve apostles. So they were eye-witnesses of all that they record in their Gospels: His teaching, His miracles, His crucifixion and His appearances after He had risen from the dead. St Mark was a companion and 'secretary' of St Peter (St Peter was the chief of the twelve apostles.) St Luke was the companion of St Paul, who had met Jesus after He had risen from the dead.

These four Gospels are authentic. There is no good reason to deny that they were really written by Saints Matthew, Mark, Luke and John. No scholar today denies that they're written in the style of Greek commonly spoken in Palestine in the first century of our era. They show a perfect awareness of the complicated situation of Palestine at that time: they know all about the various groups within Judaism and the tangled relations of the Jewish and Roman authorities. The gospel-writers also give us details about Jerusalem, now verified by archaeology, which show that they knew the city before it was utterly destroyed in AD 70.

There are far more manuscripts of the four Gospels than of any other ancient work. For example, there are ten times as many ancient manuscripts describing the life of Christ as there are describing the life of Julius Caesar. If one wanted to deny that the Gospels give us a reliable picture of Christ, one would have to deny that we know anything at all about ancient history.

The Gospels never contradict each other. They give

us four different portraits of the public life of Jesus Christ, with a few details about His birth and boyhood. So while it's true that they have different emphases, it's not true that they're incompatible. For example, St John likes to recounts the debates that Christ had in Jerusalem with those who were 'experts' in the Jewish Law. The other three gospel-writers concentrate more on Christ's preaching to ordinary people, in the smaller towns and villages outside Jerusalem. But they all agree that Christ preached to both kinds of people, and that He preached inside and outside Jerusalem. Sometimes it can be difficult to see how the different accounts fit together. For example, each of the gospel-writers gives us a slightly different description of whom Jesus appeared to after the Resurrection. They don't contradict each other: they just all make their own choice of which apparitions to describe. This shows that the four of them were not writing according to a pre-arranged plan — if they had been they would have avoided even these apparent discrepancies. Each one of them is an independent witness to the life, death and resurrection of Jesus Christ.

Another sign of the reliability of the Gospels is the way that the men who wrote them lived and died. What motivated them? They weren't interested in making money. Very early on, Christ had told them, 'The foxes have holes, and the birds of the air have nests, but the Son of Man [He means Himself] has nowhere to lay his head.' They knew that following Christ was not the way to have an easy life. St John had been a fisherman, St Matthew a tax-gatherer, St Luke a physician, but they gave up their livelihoods to preach the news of Christ's Resurrection. They didn't marry. They didn't seek power or influence: in fact, they were persecuted for their preaching, thrown into prison or put to death. Why were they willing to go through all this? Because they knew the truth of what they had seen and heard. They put up with all that happened to them in imitation of Christ, 'who when He was reviled, did not revile; when He suffered, He threatened not'. They knew that just as Jesus rose again on the third day, so they would live with Him if they persevered in bearing witness to Him.

Jesus Christ left behind Him a community, of which the twelve apostles were, so to speak, the pillars. To join the community, one had to be admitted either by one of the apostles or by one of their successors (this is still the case today.) This community, as you know, is called 'the Church', and it has always recognized the four Gospels as being the only four authentic accounts of what Christ did during His life on earth. This rules out the possibility that our Gospels could have been changed since they were first written. From the first generation of Christianity, the Church has been spread across many different lands and cities, and wherever the Church has been established, the four Gospels have been read. It's impossible that anyone could have even acquired all the copies of the Gospels, let alone have changed them all without anyone noticing or objecting!

Later on, after the apostles had died, and the name of 'Jesus' had become well-known even among people who didn't belong to the Church, some philosophers used this Name to gain credence for their own, non-Christian ideas. For example, some of them thought that the human body is evil, and they pretended that Jesus had said the same. Some of them made up sayings that they attributed to Him, and pretended that they had been handed down secretly from one of the apostles. And so they wrote works that they called, for example, 'the Gospel of Thomas' and even 'the Gospel of Judas' (Judas was the apostle who *betrayed* Jesus!) But no one in the Church was fooled by this: and when the ideas of these philosophers ceased being fashionable, their works mostly disappeared, as nobody wanted to read them any more. These are what you've heard described as the 'apocryphal gospels'. No one knows who wrote them, but we know that it wasn't the apostles or their disciples. The apostles' works were treasured by the early Church, just as they are treasured by the Church today, whereas these 'apocryphal' works were rejected by the successors of the apostles as spurious.

But finally, don't just take my word for the trustworthiness of the Gospels. Try reading one of them for yourself. Why not begin with St Matthew's Gospel, reading perhaps a chapter a day? You'll see for yourself that it just tells a calm, sensible story – astonishing of course, in many of its details, but not written in a strange or preposterous way. And ask yourself: why would anyone *say* all this, if it weren't true?

With best wishes,
Christophorus

Letter Six

ON JESUS CHRIST

Dear Ali,

I'm glad that you've started reading the Gospel of St Matthew. Let me know of any questions that come to mind as you go through it.

I promised to write in this letter about Jesus Christ. But I won't talk about His miracles, as you can find those described for yourself, as you read the Gospels. I want to talk about who He seems to be. Remember, I'm not asking you to accept that the Gospels are inspired by God, even though I believe this as a Catholic. I'm just asking you to approach them as important historical documents, as you might approach a life of Napoleon written by some of his closest officers.

Notice first of all the simple goodness of Jesus Christ. From the moment He left His home in Nazareth and began His public ministry, His whole life was spent helping others. He preached, healed and taught. The nights He gave to prayer. He never once complains about the enormous numbers of peoples coming to Him with requests; He never refuses to help anyone who sincerely asks for help. He never tells a lie. He is entirely pure. Nor does He ever do anything that He later regrets.

He lives His whole life in obedience to God, whom

He calls His Father. When some of His disciples think to prevent His arrest by drawing their swords, He says, 'Shall I not drink the chalice that the Father has given me?' All His teaching aims at helping people to trust in God, and to live their lives for God's glory.

Normally speaking, everyone who believes in God will, at times, ask God to have mercy on him, or to forgive him his sins. But Jesus never does either of these things, since He has no sins to be forgiven. In fact, He says to the people who want to have Him killed, 'Which of you convicts me of sin?' No one answers.

He was patient even with the people who put Him to death. At His trial He was slandered and scourged and beaten and crowned with thorns, but He didn't threaten the men who did these things, nor call down curses upon them – though He does solemnly warn Caiaphas the high-priest that He, Jesus, will one day be Caiaphas's judge. When He is finally being crucified, He prays, 'Father, forgive them, for they do not know what they are doing.'

I mention all these things, Ali, simply to prove that Jesus was at the very least a good man. Whatever virtue you think of, love for the poor, obedience to God, courage, willingness to sacrifice one's own time and comfort for others, goodness even to one's enemies, Jesus Christ possessed these virtues in an astonishing degree.

But secondly, notice His wisdom. It's not simply that all His actions are good; all His words are wise. He never has to correct Himself, or retract anything that He's already said. He never changes His mind about the content of the message that He has from God.

As you read through the Gospels, you'll see the

beautiful parables that Christ uses to explain who God is, such as the parable of the Good Samaritan or the Prodigal Son. I dare say that particular phrases will stick in your mind: 'Blessed are the pure in heart, for they shall see God'; 'Love your enemies, do good to them that hate you'; 'What does it profit a man if he gain the whole world and suffer the loss of his own soul?'; 'Render to Caesar the things that are Caesar's, and to God the things that are God's'; 'You cannot serve God and mammon'; 'Lay not up for yourselves treasures on earth, where the rust and moth consume and thieves break through and steal; but lay up for yourselves treasures in heaven', 'Where your treasure is, there also is your heart'. I don't know which of Christ's words will make the deepest impression on you, but I know that you'll see that He was astonishingly wise as well as good. You'll also see how the intellectual elite of Jerusalem constantly tried to catch Him out with their questions, or at least make Him hesitate in His answers, but that no one ever could.

Nothing I've said so far is meant to prove that Christ was more than a man. Yet since He was both wise and good, we must pay careful attention to what His words suggest about who He is. He is a man, certainly: He often refers to Himself as 'the Son of Man', as it were emphasizing His human nature. But that in itself is interesting – after all, why should someone feel the need to emphasize his human nature, if he were only a man and nothing else? You and I don't go round telling people that we're human beings, since it's perfectly obvious that we are.

But many of Jesus's words indicate that although He is really a man, the Son of the Virgin Mary, He is something more as well. For example, He says, 'No man comes to the Father except by me.' Could someone who was merely a man make such a staggering claim? And just before these words, He says, 'I am the way, the truth and the life.' A mere man, or someone who was just a prophet, might well claim to speak the truth, or even to be 'God's mouthpiece'. But he would never claim to *be* the truth in person.

Or again, when Jesus says, 'Whoever loses his life for my sake, will find it', don't His words suggest that He is something more than just a man? How could any mere man promise that people would find eternal life provided that they laid down their lives on his behalf?

Throughout the Gospel we see that Christ forgives sins. He doesn't just pray that people's sins will be forgiven; He grants them forgiveness on His own authority and then tells them to go in peace. Can a mere man do this? At another time He says that He will judge the nations, dividing the sheep from the goats. But more than this: He says that those who were kind to or maltreated the needy, were kind to or maltreated *Him*. How can this be?

Consider also how confidently He adds to the Law that God had given in the Old Testament to the Jews: 'You have heard that it was said to the men of old, *Thou shalt not kill*. But I say to you, that whoever is angry with His brother shall be in danger of the judgment . . . You have heard that it was said to them of old, *Thou shalt not commit adultery*. But I say to you, that whoever shall look on a woman to lust after her, has already committed adultery with her in his heart.' He speaks as if He had the same authority as God had in giving the ten commandments.

By saying and doing things like this, Jesus allows His hearers to understand that although He is a man, He is something more as well. Some of His statements are even more explicit. Once when He was debating with the Jews of Jerusalem, the name of Abraham was mentioned. After saying that Abraham himself had looked forward with great eagerness to the times that had now arrived, Christ says, 'Amen, Amen I say to you: before Abraham was made, I am.' On another occasion, He said to the Jews, 'I and the Father are one.'

So in the four Gospels, which are factual accounts of Christ's life, we find a man who claims to be more that just a man. The apostles knew Jesus Christ intimately: they went with Him everywhere. They knew that He was truly human. But from the things that He did and said, they saw that He was also something more. As the angel said, announcing His birth, 'He shall be called Emmanuel – a name that means, God is with us.'

With best wishes,

Christophorus

Letter Seven

ON THE INCARNATION

Dear Ali,

You complain that I didn't make it clear in my last letter who we say that Jesus Christ is. But I think in fact that you've guessed rightly, because you finish by asking, 'How can a man be God? Or how can God die?'

Yes, we firmly believe that Christ as well as being truly a man is also truly God: He is 'the Word made flesh', as the apostle St John says. You ask how this can be. I'll answer with one of Jesus's own sayings, 'All things are possible for God.' God is almighty, as we both believe. Therefore He can do whatever He wants, provided it's not incompatible with His own goodness. If God wants to, He's able to become Man: if He wasn't able to do this, He wouldn't be all-powerful.

But you must understand that when we talk about God becoming a man, we don't mean that one thing turns into another. The Word, the Second Person of the Holy Trinity, did not and cannot stop being God. The divine nature can't be changed into anything else. No: but it can take something else to itself. And that's what happened at the great event that Christians call 'the Incarnation'. God the Word took to Himself a human nature, so that He could be born into this world as a human child.

This explains some of Jesus' mysterious sayings in the Gospel. How could someone who'd been born some thirty years ago from a human mother say 'Before Abraham was made, I am'? Or how could a mere man say, 'The Father and I are one'? If Jesus had only had a human nature, even a sinless human nature, these sayings wouldn't have been true. But if He possesses the divine nature as well; if He is God as well as man, then we can understand them. He existed 'before' Abraham, because He was God even when Abraham was not yet born. He is 'one' with the Father, because the Father and the Word possess one and the same divine nature.

Christians don't believe that Jesus Christ is a 'mixture' of God and man, like one of the demi-gods you might read about in Greek mythology. He's not half-god and half-man. It wouldn't make any sense to talk about someone being 'half-god', since God has no parts. No, Christ is really a man, like you or me, but He is also truly God. He's the Son of God from all eternity, and the Son of Mary since the year AD 1.

I think you may even find in the Koran a suggestion of the divinity of Christ. Doesn't it say that 'Christ is a spirit proceeding from God' (Sura 4:171) and a 'Word from Himself' (Sura 3:45)? If Christ is a spirit, He must be more than just man, since men aren't spirits. Or again, how can a mere man *be* 'a word from God'? A word expresses what something is. So if Christ by His very nature expresses what God is, He must be more than just a man.

Do you remember that when I spoke about the mystery of the Holy Trinity, I said that God is three Persons 'in' one nature? In the mystery of the Incarnation, it's almost the opposite that we have to say: Christ is one Person in two natures. He is one person, namely, the Second Person of the Holy Trinity, God the Word or God the Son. But He has two natures. He has the divine nature that is His from all eternity, and He has the human nature that He took from the holy Virgin Mary.

It's right for us, my friend, to be amazed at such things. For who could have guessed or even dreamed that they were possible, had God not brought them to pass? Christ Himself knew that people would be astonished when it dawned on them who He was. That's why He let people perceive His identity slowly, by His many miracles and by His enigmatic sayings. He didn't want them to be so astonished that they'd refuse to believe.

It's right, I say, that we should be astonished to think that Christ might be both God and man: but it's not right to be so astonished that *we* should refuse to believe. He proved by His goodness and wisdom that He was trustworthy. He proved by His many miracles that God, whom He called His Father, was with Him. And so we must believe Him when He tells us who He is.

I think you've read this passage in St Matthew's Gospel:

> And Jesus came into the quarters of Caesarea Philippi, and he asked his disciples, saying: 'Who do men say that the Son of Man is?'
>
> But they said: 'Some, John the Baptist; and others, Elijah, and others Jeremiah, or one of the prophets.'
>
> Jesus says to them: 'But who do you say that I am?'
>
> Simon Peter answered and said: 'You are Christ, the Son of the Living God'.
>
> And Jesus said to him, 'Blessed are you, Simon bar-Jona: because flesh and blood has not revealed it to you, but my

Father who is in Heaven.

Jesus acknowledges the truth of what Peter says: He is the Son of the Living God. He is not just a prophet or teacher; He is God Himself, come in the flesh. He is the Word, eternally begotten of the Father.

You ask, 'How can God die?' But remember that Jesus Christ is also truly human. He was as human as you or me. His divine nature doesn't swallow up His humanity. The two natures are united in the one Person, and each of them has what belongs to it by right. Now it's a property of human nature to be able to die, because we each have a body and a soul, and death is simply the separation of one from the other. Jesus too had a body and soul, and so He too was able to die. His divine nature didn't die, of course, since the divine nature is unchangeable. He didn't die *as* God, but *as* man. Yet He who died, Jesus Christ, is truly God, so in this sense we can say that God was born, and died and rose again.

We are astonished at this; and yet, should we be quite so astonished? It belongs to God to do wonderful things, after all, and what could be more wonderful than this? Or put it this way: don't good people long to share what they have with others? But then why shouldn't God, who is surpassingly good, desire to share His own self in a surpassing way? This is what happened in the Incarnation: God shared His own nature with a human nature so completely that they are only one Person.

Do you wonder, perhaps, if it isn't demeaning for God to come into His own creation like this? I've heard people object to the Catholic faith, saying: 'Surely God lessens His own majesty by uniting it to our lowly human nature!' But do you remember, when I was talking about the Holy Trinity, I said that God's 'oneness' is seen to be greater than any other 'oneness' in that not even there being three divine Persons can cause there to be more than one divine nature? I'd say something similar here. God's majesty is so great, and His holiness is so perfect, that it cannot be lessened by anything, not even by His being born as a little child. The Incarnation doesn't only show us how good God is, that He came to earth to save us: it also shows us how powerful He is. He's able to become a man without ceasing to be God, and without losing anything of His majesty. He's so powerful that he can live as one of us, and yes, even suffer and die.

With best wishes,
Christophorus

Letter Eight

ON THE RESURRECTION

Dear Ali,

You say that you are still thinking over what I wrote in my last letter. I'm happy to hear it: but don't forget to pray too. Ask God to show you where the truth is, and to show you what His will for you is. He'll help you to understand what you're reading in the Gospel.

But your main question was about the Resurrection: 'Can we be sure', you wrote, 'that Jesus Christ rose again from the dead; or did He rise, perhaps, in some spiritual way, but not with His physical body? And anyway, can we be sure that He had really died first?'

The Catholic faith is this: that Jesus Christ really did rise again on the third day, with that very same body that had been nailed to the Cross by order of Pontius Pilate, and that He is now living in a glorified state with this same body and will be for ever.

This is the faith of Christians: but it's also, I'd suggest, the only thing that makes sense of the historical facts related in the Gospels and in other early Christian books, like the 'Acts of the Apostles'. In the first place, Jesus was really crucified. Several times in the course of the Gospel He predicts His coming death, as well as His Resurrection. He says, for example, 'I have power to lay down my life and I have power to take it up again: this commandment I have received from my Father.' All His twelve apostles were with Him when He was arrested. St Peter, the first of the apostles, and St John, who was especially dear to Christ, were present during His trial. As He walked to the Cross, St Luke tells us that 'a great multitude of people lamented Him', and that He spoke in particular to the women, saying: 'Daughters of Jerusalem, weep not for me; but weep for yourselves and for your children' – because He knew that within a generation, Jerusalem would be destroyed. As He hung on the cross, St Matthew and St Mark tell us that 'a great multitude' of those who had ministered to Him in Galilee saw Him die. St John tells us that Christ's own mother, Mary, stood at the foot of the Cross, and that Christ gave her into the care of 'the beloved disciple' who stood with her (this was St John himself). So there's no room for doubt that it really was He who suffered on the Cross.

St Matthew, St Mark and St Luke tell us that a miracle took place when Jesus died: the 'veil of the temple' – the thick curtain secluding the most holy place of the Jewish temple – was torn in two, from top to bottom. Finally, a Roman centurion drove his lance right through Christ's side into His heart, to verify that He was indeed dead. St John, the beloved disciple, saw this with his own eyes. As well as this, the secular historians whom I mentioned in an earlier letter also testify to the Crucifixion. If anything is a fact of history, it's the death of Jesus Christ.

Now, what are the next facts that we can establish, approaching the question as impartial observers? It's certain that Christ's followers, those who had come down with Him from Galilee to Jerusalem, who had seen

Him captured and crucified, were very soon afterwards preaching to the people of Jerusalem that His tomb was empty and that they had seen Him alive. There are only three possibilities: either those who claimed to have seen the risen Christ were deliberately trying to fool others; or they were mistaken in what they claimed to have seen; or they were telling the simple truth. In other words either the apostles were deceivers, or they were deceived – or else Christ was (and is) truly risen. So which is it to be?

First of all, could the apostles have been deceivers? It is possible that one person might tell a lie just for the sake if it, but for many people to enter into a conspiracy to lie and to maintain this lie until death, requires some very strong motive. What motive could the apostles have had for such a thing? I've mentioned in an earlier letter that there was no wealth or political power to be gained from preaching the Resurrection in the first century AD. The apostles, except for St John, were all martyred.

Could they have been seeking revenge over the authorities who'd crucified their Lord and Master? To try to gain a mere appearance of revenge by preaching as risen someone whom one knows to be dead, and to maintain the pretence, year after year, in city after city, and finally to die for it would be literally insane. But can twelve madmen found an organisation that lasts for centuries? Or is a bitter grief, carried to the point of madness, or an angry iteration of what one knows to be a lie, attractive? Can it convert hearts, so that thousands of new believers become ready to die for One whom they've never seen?

Read St Peter's speeches in the Acts of the Apostles, or

his letters, or the letters of St John and St James. I'm sure that they won't seem to you like products of mad men or liars. A mad man or a pathological liar could hardly have conceived such sublime thoughts as these: 'God is light, and in Him there is no darkness', 'the world passes away, and the desire of the world; but he who does the will of God abides forever', 'We look for a new heaven and a new earth, in which justice dwells', 'The anger of man does not work the justice of God', 'Let those who suffer according to God's will do right and entrust their souls to a faithful Creator'. And there are many such beautiful things in their letters.

Again, think of St Paul. He'd not been a friend of Jesus before the Crucifixion. In fact, he was just the opposite. When the twelve apostles began to preach, he was their principal opponent, a fierce persecutor of the Church. But later he astonished everyone by saying that he'd met the risen Christ. He spent the rest of his life on endless missionary journeys to spread the news of the Resurrection to as many countries as possible, until he was eventually beheaded by the imperial authorities at Rome. What possible motive could he have had for labouring so hard to spread a lie? No, the apostles weren't liars who exploited gullible people.

Could the witnesses to the Resurrection have been simply mistaken? They weren't mistaken about the empty tomb. They had seen where the body of Jesus was laid, and that it was empty on the Sunday morning. There are few facts of history, certainly of ancient history, which have as many independent witnesses as does the empty tomb. Neither the Jewish authorities nor the Roman soldiers could deny something which was notorious to the whole of Jerusalem. This is why the Jewish authorities bribed the Roman soldiers to say that the apostles had stolen Jesus' body by night. If the tomb hadn't been empty, the authorities would simply have recovered the body and put it on show.

But could the apostles' meetings, at least, with their risen Lord have been simple hallucinations? It's true that those who've been bereaved of one whom they dearly loved may sometimes fancy that they see that person again when they glimpse the face of some stranger. But this is not what the Gospels describe. They tell us of Christ appearing to whole groups at a time, talking to them at length, being touched by them and even eating with them. These stories were not made up by other men, later on: St Matthew and St John were among the twelve apostles, and each of them recounts how Jesus appeared to the whole group of apostles after His Resurrection.

Again, granted that one person can have a hallucination during a time of fever or when his mind is in some way unhinged, can eleven healthy men all have repeated hallucinations over a period of forty days, with all eleven seeing and hearing the same thing each time? Isn't this rather harder to believe than the Resurrection itself? Remember too how slow the apostles were to believe: their first reaction when the woman told them of the empty tomb was that it was mere nonsense – until they'd gone to see for themselves. And even when the other apostles told him that they had seen Jesus again, the apostle Thomas refused to believe until he'd actually touched the places where the nails had gone through His hands. The apostles weren't credulous; they were working men of ordinary common sense.

So I believe, Ali, that a truly impartial historian who approaches the Gospels with an open mind can come to only one conclusion: the apostles must have been telling the truth when they said that they had seen Jesus Christ risen again, after He had been crucified.

With best wishes,

Christophorus

Letter Nine

ON CHRIST'S DEATH

Dear Ali,

I found one remark in your last letter very interesting: you said that it is not Christ's Resurrection which seems to you hard to believe, but rather His death. Of course you know that the former wouldn't have been possible without the latter. But I suppose what you mean is that you can't understand why Christ should have allowed Himself to die. 'You claim that He is truly God', you wrote to me, 'but God is always more powerful than man. So how could He have been overcome by men? Or if He was the Son of God, why did God allow Him to be so humiliated as to die on a Cross, like a slave?'

I don't think you should be so surprised that Jesus Christ was put to death by His fellow-countrymen. The prophets who came before Him were persecuted by their fellow Jews and finally put to death (you can find this mentioned by the Koran as well, in Sura 2:61.) So it shouldn't be so surprising that Jesus Christ, who though more than just a prophet was nevertheless the prophet *par excellence*, was also killed.

But your question does lead us to one important truth. Christ couldn't have been killed, by the Jews or the Romans or anyone else, unless He'd first chosen to die.

After all, He raised several people to life in the course of His ministry, so He could surely have prevented His own death, had He so desired. No: Christ's death was *voluntary*. So the prophet Isaiah, writing about 700 years before the event, made this prediction: 'He was offered because He willed it' (by the way, the prophets often use the past tense even when they're speaking of future events, because something God has decided on is as unchangeable as if it were already in the past).

Don't misunderstand me, though: Jesus Christ's death wasn't a form of suicide. It's always a sin to kill oneself or to ask others to kill oneself. Jesus didn't ask the Jewish or Roman authorities to kill Him, nor did He taunt them until they did. Rather He *foresaw* that His preaching and His miracles would lead the authorities to seek His death, and He didn't try to avoid this, because He knew that He'd come into the world for one thing above all else: to die for the world.

We can't hope to grasp all the reasons why Jesus had to die for the world, but we can give some explanation of it. In one sense, it was to prepare for the Resurrection. He couldn't rise again unless He'd first died, and His rising again was the way Christ proved that all He'd taught was true. For example, His Resurrection showed the truth of all that He he'd said or hinted about His own identity. It shows that He is the Son of God.

But there's more to Christ's death than this. It wasn't merely a tunnel along which He had to pass in order to reach the Resurrection. It has a value in itself. In fact, it has an infinite value. Remember that Christ's death was voluntary. His life wasn't something that men took from Him against His will. It was something that He freely gave up. Why? So that He could offer it to God His Father.

I've said that it's *as* man and not *as* God that Christ died. That's true: but He was always a divine Person, even on the Cross. So what He offered to His Father as He died was *the life of a divine Person*. There can't be anything more precious to offer than this. Christ died on the Cross, then, so that He could offer His own life as an infinitely perfect gift to His heavenly Father.

Christ would have been willing to do this simply in order to honour His Father. But in fact there was another reason as well. You've heard it said, I'm sure, that Christ came into the world to take away our sins. Now what is a sin? Isn't it a form of stealing from God? The sinner refuses to honour God by obeying His Law: he 'steals' from God some of the honour and glory that is His due. Of course God can't really suffer in Himself from anything that we do; He doesn't need our good deeds, after all. But all the same, it remains an objective fact that whoever sins commits an offence against God. Now Jesus Christ had a great desire to make up for all the sins that had ever been committed against the divine majesty. And He did this by offering to God His Father something that far outweighed all the 'thefts' that men had ever made or would ever make from God's honour. He offered up His own life.

This is what Catholics call the 'Redemption'. This means that Christ freely gave up His life for us to save us from our sins. He did this out of love: love for His heavenly Father, who is offended by sins, and love for us, who wouldn't have had forgiveness of our sins unless Christ had been willing to die for us.

So do you still think, my friend, that it was humiliating for Christ to die on the Cross? No doubt that's what Christ's enemies thought, and the solders who crucified Him. But He didn't think so. St Paul tells us that Christ 'despised the shame' of the Cross (it's the only thing that He ever did despise.) He didn't consider what men thought about His death on the Cross, because men's judgments are fallible. He only considered what God His Father 'thought' about it: and in God's sight, Jesus's death was not something shameful or humiliating, but rather the most glorious deed that has ever been done on earth, and that ever will be done until the end of time.

That's why Catholics aren't ashamed that Jesus Christ died on the Cross. On the contrary, as St Paul says, we 'glory' in the Cross. It was the means that our Saviour chose to free us from slavery to sin and to make us children of God. That's why we always begin and end our prayers by making the sign of the Cross on ourselves, while calling on the Holy Trinity, for whose glory we have been redeemed.

With best wishes,

Christophorus

Letter Ten

ON CHRIST'S DEATH
(cont'd.)

Dear Ali,

I was pleased to receive your speedy reply to my last letter. I just wish that all Christians thought about these questions as deeply as you do. But when we're brought up among wonders, it's all too easy for us to become accustomed to them. We can forget to be grateful, as if God's amazing gifts were simply our due.

You say that you still don't quite understand *why* Christ had to die to take away our sins. 'Since God is all merciful, couldn't He have just forgiven them anyway? And I wonder if it's really fair that Christ should die when it was we who'd sinned. Can God really condemn the innocent like the guilty?'

I think in part you may have got hold of a wrong idea of what we mean by the Redemption. As you know, there are some people who profess themselves to be Christians but who are not Catholics, and some of them hold notions about Christ that aren't those of the Church. For example, some of them say that God literally punished Christ for our sins; that God wanted to punish someone, and that Christ 'volunteered' to be punished instead of us.

Now this is a distorted picture of what the Catholic Church holds. God didn't literally punish His Son, for as you say, a just judge will punish only the guilty, never the innocent, and God is certainly a just judge. No, the Cross wasn't about Jesus being punished, it was about Him making a free gift of His life to His Father. And this gift, because it was given with such burning charity by one who is a divine Person, was infinitely pleasing to God. It was far more pleasing to Him than all the sins that can ever be committed from the world's beginning to its end are displeasing. God wasn't pleased by Christ's suffering and death as such: but He took delight in the free gift that Christ made of His infinitely precious life, when He let His life's blood be poured out, in witness to the truth.

Of course you're right to say that God didn't need the death of Christ to forgive our sins. In principle, God could have found some other means of granting us forgiveness, or even done it by a simple act of His will. God is free, after all. I'm not trying to show you that God *had* to choose this way to save us, just how fitting it was that He did. Since it was men who had sinned, a man died on their behalf. But since this man was more than just a man, His death had a power that no other death could possess.

You ask why God let His Son die in such a painful way, when He is all-merciful. But it's precisely because God *is* so merciful that He gave up His only Son for us like this. Because He is merciful, He wants us to believe in His love. And He knows that we'll do that more easily when we see how far He was willing to go to save us. As

St Paul says, 'God shows his love for us in that while we were yet sinners, Christ died for us.'

Next you write: 'When I forgive someone, I change my attitude towards them. Did God's attitude towards us change, then, when Jesus Christ died? If so, what of the statement that God is the necessary being, the One who can't change? It seems as though the God we reach by philosophy isn't the same as the God of the Bible.'

Well, since there's only one God, that can't be right. What's more, God is the source both of true philosophy and of the Holy Scriptures. He's the source of philosophy because He gave us the minds by which we think, and He's the source of Scripture, as we'd say, because He inspired it and then guided the Church to collect all the inspired books into one volume. So if philosophy and the Scriptures were ever in opposition, God would be contradicting Himself, which is impossible.

How shall I answer your question? First, God is certainly unchanging. Not only does philosophy teach that; the Scriptures do as well. For example, the apostle James in his letter says: 'With Him there is no variation or shadow due to change.' Yet God's 'relation' to us is said to change: not because He does, but because we do. God's nature is always the same: He is always holy, pure and just. So if a sinner is brought into the presence of God, he can't bear the difference between his own nature and God's. He experiences God's holiness as a burning judgment on himself. But if someone is made pure by God's grace, and then brought into God's presence, that man will find delight in this same holiness of God.

So it's not that God changes in Himself because of the death of Christ. It's rather that because of Christ's death, and as a 'reward', so to speak, to Christ, for the sacrifice that He made, God our Father pours out His grace on mankind so that we can be made holy. He does this for everyone who believes in the Saviour that He sent to us, and who's willing to live as Christ taught.

But God didn't suddenly decide to do all this after the Crucifixion. It was part of His eternal plan that mankind, since it had fallen by disobedience, should be saved through the perfect obedience of His Son. So God didn't change because of Christ's death; He willed from eternity that *we* should be changed by it. When He forgives us, He's not literally changing His 'attitude' towards us. He's allowing us to enter into union with Himself, so that we might one day experience His holiness as joy and not as punishment.

Yet, because it's hard for us to realise these things that are so far beyond our comprehension, Holy Scripture sometimes speaks in a way more suited to our human condition, just as mothers speak very simply when they're talking to their young children. So the prophets and others sometimes talk of God becoming angry, or forgetting His wrath, or intending to punish people for sins and then changing His mind when these people repent. But all these things are figures of speech. They mean that God's relation with us is a personal relation, that we can cut ourselves off from God by our sins, and that we're brought into union with Him by His grace and our repentance.

Finally, you write: 'What of all those who died before the time of Jesus Christ? Did they have no chance to have their sins forgiven?' They must have had an opportunity, since it says in our Scriptures, 'God wills all men to be saved and to come to the knowledge of the truth.' No one is excluded from salvation except by his own choice. And remember that God is *above* time. He's not only eternal in the sense that He had no beginning, but also in the sense that He doesn't experience the flow of time; He doesn't experience past, present and future as we do. The day of creation is present to Him, not as a memory, but as an ever-living reality. The day of judgment is present to Him, not as something to be awaited, as it is with us, but as something that He now *sees*. God has always seen Jesus's loving sacrifice of His life, and for the sake of this, He has always offered graces of repentance to mankind.

Only, since the Passion of His Son, two things have changed. First, heaven has been opened to man, so that those who die as God's friends can now enter heaven to be with Him, rather than resting in hope. Secondly, graces are offered much more abundantly to mankind now than they were before Christ died. Before the Cross, grace was on earth like a stream through which a man might wade; now it is like a mighty torrent which none can cross.

With best wishes,
Christophorus

Letter Eleven

ON THE FALL OF MAN

Dear Ali,

I was wondering if you would notice my reference to mankind as 'fallen' and, of course, you did. You write: 'Do Christians really believe in the Fall as an historical event? I thought that most of them nowadays said that it was something symbolic, just a way of speaking about how easily people sin. But if you take it literally, how can you reconcile it with what science tells us about evolution? In any case, how could babies be born with a sin on account of what an ancestor of theirs did long ago? It hardly seems compatible with God's justice.'

First of all, then, and whatever you may have heard to the contrary, the Catholic Church firmly believes in the Fall of Man as a real event that took place at the beginning of history. God created one man and one woman in harmony with Himself, with each other and with the world around them. He put 'grace' into their souls, which means that His Holy Spirit was within them, making them holy.

God let our first parents be 'tested'. This was really a way for them to prove themselves worthy of His friendship. He wanted them to come like this to a greater glory that He had in store for them. But instead they tried to make themselves independent of Him. They broke His solemn commandment about eating the forbidden fruit; and so they lost God's friendship, as well as the harmony that He'd placed in their human nature. And even though Scripture tells us that the man at least repented (and we can hope that the woman did as well), their children and descendants down to the end of the world are born lacking this harmony in their soul and body. We're all born liable to sin and death and not yet friends of God.

That is the Catholic doctrine of the Fall of Man. I hope you can see how closely it's linked to our belief in the Redemption. God had intended our first parents to inherit eternal life at the end of their time on earth. If they'd been faithful to Him, they would have entered heaven without even having to die. They were 'heirs' to God's own glory. When they sinned, they lost that inheritance and by the same stroke disinherited their offspring. So Christ came into the world to repair the friendship between man and God. The 'reward' that He earned for mankind was the recovery of eternal life. By His death, Christ *merited* this for all of mankind; though each individual man or woman needs to accept it in person, to become a child of God and an heir to heaven.

You ask how one, far-off sin could have such enormous consequences, down from one end of history to the other. I agree that it's a mystery. But it's not arbitrary. In fact, it's a sign of how much God honoured our first parents. God wanted them to co-operate with Him in His work of creation. This was true in a physical sense first of all. By coming together in marital love, the man and woman would become the father and mother of the whole human race. But God also wanted to confer a *spiritual* fatherhood and motherhood upon them. He gave them a power, insofar as human beings can have it, to *pass on the holiness* that they'd received from Him. The grace that He'd given to them was so abundant that it didn't only sanctify their minds. It sanctified their very bodies, with all their physical powers, including their power of procreation. So if they'd remained faithful they would have begotten children in the power of God's grace, and those children would have been holy from the beginning.

But when our first parents (alas!) turned away from the Holy Trinity, the only source of good, they lost these good things. They lost their friendship with God, since they'd deliberately broken His command. And they lost the grace which had sanctified their souls and bodies, because the Holy Spirit doesn't remain with those who defy Him. Don't think of the Fall as a few branches lopped off a tree; it was more like the tree itself being pulled up by the roots. And just as when a tree is torn up by the roots all the surrounding earth is shaken and scattered, so when grace was plucked up from deep within that first man and woman, their natural powers were all wounded by the rupture. Their power of procreation was wounded too. It was no longer sanctified by God's grace.

So now, when they came together as man and wife, though they could still co-operate with God to produce new life, it was a fallen power of procreation that was at work. It was as a fallen man and woman that they came together, and so their offspring also were fallen in God's eyes, and born without His grace.

Do you see that it's because God honoured the first

man and woman so highly that their sin affects us? If God hadn't given them the power to beget children in holiness, their sin would have concerned themselves alone. But because He loved them and gave them a power to pass on holiness to their children, their sin does affect us. Once they had lost holiness themselves, they could no longer pass it on to their offspring.

I think I can hear you about to ask me, 'But why did God do things in this way? Couldn't He have created every new generation of human beings to be as perfect as Adam and Eve in the beginning, and let each individual person be tested as those two were?' Of course He could, had He chosen to. But that would have meant taking away from our first parents the possibility of being our parents in a spiritual sense as well as in a physical one. And He didn't want to deprive them of this honour. As it says somewhere in our Scriptures, 'He honours the parents above the children': because the parents reflect His own glory as creator of the universe.

Perhaps you will say, 'Yet God could have ordained things so that if Adam and Eve didn't fall, they would have passed on His grace to their children, but if they did, the next generation would still have been created in grace all the same.' Again, He could have done, but He didn't choose to. The testing of Adam and his wife wasn't a game, so that God might say like a child playing with his fellows, 'That time didn't count.' Our actions have consequences, and God honours us by letting our free actions, even when they're bad, produce their natural fruit – though His mercy always intervenes to lessen the evil in some way.

Original sin, of course, isn't *personal* sin. A new-born

baby is incapable of committing any personal sin. Original sin isn't an action but an absence. It's the absence of the grace that should have been in the new-born child's soul, caused by the fallen state of his parents' power of procreation. So God doesn't blame the child for being born in original sin; and yet that child remains deprived of his inheritance until God's grace finds its way back into his soul. This is what happens in baptism, when water is poured upon the child's head and the Name of the Holy Trinity is invoked. At that moment, God's Holy Spirit comes to dwell in the child's soul and he becomes a child of God, like Adam and Eve before the Fall. And though he doesn't have all that harmony which our first parents enjoyed in the beginning, he has the inheritance of eternal life, and heaven stands open to him.

Doesn't it say in the Koran that Adam was driven out of Paradise for approaching the forbidden tree (Sura 2:35-6)? If this had only been a personal sin of his, with no consequences for his offspring, why should his offspring also have to live outside Paradise? But since all men are certainly born outside Paradise, all of us must have been implicated in some way in Adam's sin. Now you know how this is, according to the Catholic faith.

I've run out of space! So I'll have to deal with your question about evolution next time.

With best wishes,

Christophorus

Letter Twelve

ON SCIENCE AND
THE FALL OF MAN

Dear Ali,

I'm glad that my explanation of original sin made sense to you. But you still want to know whether what the Church teaches about human origins is compatible with what science says about them.

For a Catholic, there's no danger of a contradiction between our faith and any human discovery. Do you remember how I said that true philosophy couldn't contradict the Scriptures, since both have their origin in God? It's just the same here. Any scientific discoveries that men make are due to their God-given reason, and so they can't contradict what the Scriptures say. If ever they seem to, this either means that someone has misunderstood the Scriptures (I don't mean the Church, since the Catholic Church as a whole can never misunderstand her own writings, but some individual person), or else that someone is mistaken about what they think has been discovered.

The next point to make is that 'science', by which people today normally mean conclusions drawn from experiments made on the material world, can't possibly either prove or disprove the Fall of Man. The reason is that the Fall of Man, as taught by the Church, was a one-off event. It's a 'contingent truth' – something that might not have happened, but did. Now science doesn't establish contingent truths, but necessary ones. The true objects of scientific discovery are the properties of material things and the laws governing their interaction. For example, it is a scientific discovery that water boils at 212 degrees Fahrenheit, or that force equals mass times acceleration. But the temperature of the water in my bath this morning or the force with which I shut my front door last Monday are not proper objects of scientific study. They are one-off realities, now finished and gone. The only normal way in which someone could have a well-founded certainty about them is by having been present at the time, able to put a thermometer in the bath or to measure the speed with which the door slammed shut (I say the only 'normal' way, because of course God could, if He wished, reveal these truths to someone in a supernatural way).

Now in this respect, the Fall of Man is like the temperature of my bath-water, not like the laws of motion. The only natural way in which anyone could know that it had occurred would be by having witnessed it, and noticing the change that took place in the man and the woman. Now, however, it's not possible for anyone, whether a biologist, anthropologist or anyone else, to prove it or disprove it. Only God can reveal it, since He was there (it's true that somebody once said, 'Original sin is the only Christian dogma that is proved by experience', but that was really a joke, though a profound one). Not of course that God just revealed it 'out of the blue'. Ever since the Fall actually happened, His Spirit has preserved the memory of it among those whom He's chosen to be His witnesses to the rest of mankind. First, the sons of Seth, Adam's own son; later, the sons of Abraham; and now His own 'sons', who are born of water and the Holy Spirit.

Perhaps your difficulty is not about the Fall as such, but rather the descent of the whole race from just one man and woman, those whom we call Adam and Eve. Could this be put in doubt by scientific discoveries? Again, no, and for the same reason. That a single man and woman are the origin of the whole race is a contingent fact, not a law of nature. For example, let's suppose that the earliest human bones found in the earth seemed to belong to human beings living in several different places at the same time. Would that disprove our descent from a single couple? No, for it wouldn't be possible to show that these were the bones of the *earliest* human beings ever to have lived, since the bones of the earliest human beings might have wholly perished. So even if such findings were far more extensive and easy of interpretation than they really are, they would never confirm or refute the doctrine of descent from a single couple.

But maybe it's neither the doctrine of the Fall nor our shared descent from one man and woman which is troubling you, but rather how that first couple came into being. You write, 'Virtually all scientists believe that human beings evolved from a lower species, yet the Bible says that they were created directly by God, the man from the ground, and the woman from the man.'

Once more, the origin of the first couple is a contingent fact no longer observable. It doesn't fall within the proper domain of empirical science. If I were to forgot all I know from revelation, and someone were to ask me, 'Did the first human body come from the womb of an inferior species, or directly from the earth?', I should reply, 'Whichever it is, it must have happened by a special intervention of God, since a lower thing can't bring forth a higher one by itself; but beyond that, there's no possible way of knowing *how* it happened, so long after the event.'

It's true, as you say, that a majority of those who teach biology probably believe that our bodies evolved from some other species (though there are distinguished exceptions, perhaps more than you realise). But I wonder if they really believe this *as* biologists, or for some other reason. What I mean is this: if we've been told something repeatedly from early youth by all those in positions of authority or influence over us, such as parents, teachers, and those who control the means of mass communication; or, even more, if such people have not only affirmed a certain doctrine to be true, but have confidently treated it as a fundamental principle by which other assertions may be tested in view of their acceptance or rejection, then the doctrine in question will usually be very widely held even if it is supported by little or no solid evidence. As a certain tyrant once said, 'Most people do not have critical minds.'

Now I'd suggest that this applies rather exactly to the theory of evolution, and in particular to the theory of the evolution of the human body. There've been interesting discoveries of old bones here and there that may or may not have been human. There've been vast amounts of speculation on the significance of such finds; and the impression has been given that the fact of human evolution is certain, only its manner in doubt. In reality, there's no solid proof that any species now existing on the earth developed from a truly distinct species, nor that the human body evolved from some ape-like creature. The theory of evolution is indeed held by many scientists, but as an axiom not a conclusion; it's used to interpret data, it's not drawn from them.

That's what I should say about evolution simply as a rational animal who tries to keep his wits about him, but as a Christian I should say more. For the Scriptures, as you say, give us an account of human origins, and the Catholic Church holds that everything affirmed by Holy Scripture is true. We say that the Church has the right to interpret Scripture, but the Church can't *force* the sense of Scripture to suit modern 'scientific' opinion. For we hold that everything affirmed in Scripture is true *in precisely the sense that its human author meant when he wrote it.*

So, what does the Church, as the interpreter of Scripture, teach about our origins? First, she teaches that the human soul didn't evolve. A new human soul is created directly by God *whenever* a new person comes into being. This is true of the children who are conceived today, and it was true of the first man and woman. God creates a soul from nothing for every new human person. In fact even philosophy tells us that the soul can't have evolved. The soul is something spiritual, not something with material parts. This means that it's either there or it's not; you can't have half a soul.

As for the body, the Church has not as of the present date (AD 2009) officially forbidden Catholics from believing that this evolved from some earlier living thing. So some Catholics imagine that when the Scriptures record that

God created man from the dust of the ground, this is a kind of shorthand, as if to say, lower animals came from basic elements, and man's body gradually evolved from lower animals. If you want my personal opinion, then it's this. I find it very unlikely that the author of this part of Scripture – Moses, by tradition – had this 'shorthand' idea in mind. I think that if you'd suggested it to him as a possible meaning of his words, he would have rejected it. I also think that the tradition of the Church is so contrary to such an interpretation that she may even reject it officially one day. But that hasn't happened yet.

I hope that answers your questions! Keep them coming.

With best wishes,
Christophorus

Letter Thirteen

ON THE LOVE OF GOD

Dear Ali,

You say you'd like to know what Christians mean when they speak of the love of God. But first you ask why I spoke of the Church as 'she' in my last letter. Do we think of the Church as a woman?, you ask. Yes, in a sense we do. At least, we think of the Church as being our mother (it's a very ancient idea – you can find it in St Paul.) The baptism by which someone becomes a Christian is like a second birth: a spiritual birth, of course, not a physical one. God freely begets us as His children, by giving us His Holy Spirit. So the Church is like a Mother, because she provides the waters of baptism upon which the Holy Spirit descends. When we've been baptized, we're children of the Church, as well as children of God. We even have a saying, 'no one can have God for his Father who does not have the Church for his mother.'

But of course it's this very question of God as our Father which is causing you difficulties. You say, 'I understand that when Christians talk about God as a Father, either begetting His Word in eternity, or making human beings into His sons and daughters, they're not speaking of physical fatherhood. But even so, can any human being call God his Father? Isn't there an infinite distance between a creature and the One who creates? If God is infinitely above us, I don't see how we can call Him our Father. And can God truly love a creature as a father loves his child? A father will be sad if his son turns out badly. But we can't talk about God being sad, since sadness is a form of imperfection. So how can God be a father?'

Many questions! Let me start by trying to explain how God loves us, and then go on to say how we can love Him and even call Him, 'Father'. Actually, this order corresponds to how things are. The apostle St John says, 'Let us therefore love God, *because God first has loved us*'.

Let's begin by distinguishing two forms of love. In one sense, we love something when we want to have it, or keep it, to be fulfilled in some way. At the lowest level, this is the love that someone might have for food, or for sport. Someone 'loves fish and chips', or they 'love tennis', not because they want fish and chips or tennis in order to be happy (what would that mean?), but because they are made happy by these things. You can also have this kind of love for a person; you can want to be happy by being with a particular person. It's not always selfish, by the way, to have this kind of love, because it's a part of our nature to need other things or other people to be happy, and it's not a sin to act according to our nature. On the other hand, a relationship with another person that was *only* motivated by this sort of love would surely be selfish.

Now God can't literally have this kind of love – let's call it a 'needy love' – for creatures. Why not? Because, as you say, God has no needs. He's infinitely blessed in

Himself, and so He can't be fulfilled by any creature. But there's another kind of love. I said a moment ago that a relationship between two human beings that was based only on a 'needy love' would be something selfish. But, as I'm sure you'd agree, there are on earth friendships and marriages that are not selfish, and so there must be another kind of love as well. What is this? Quite simply, the love that seeks what is good for someone else, the love that seeks their happiness. For want of any better name, we might call this 'generous love'. We can see it especially in the affection of parents for their children.

Now this kind of love is found in God. He has a 'generous love' for all existing things. How can I be so sure? Think: He gives good things to all creatures, starting with their very existence. And He doesn't do this from any need of His own, as He has no needs. But to give good things to another without seeking to fulfil one's needs is the very definition of generous love.

In this sense we must say that God loves all things, even the rocks and stones, even the fallen spirits. Although the fallen spirits are perverse in their will, their nature is good, and they continue to have it from God. So in our Scriptures, a certain wise man says to God:

> Thou lovest all things that are, and hatest none of the things which thou hast made
>   And how could anything endure, if thou wouldst not?

But now, what kind of love can we have for God? If He were only our Creator, I suppose that we could have a love like that of a servant for a good Master, a respectful gratitude. But as you know, Christians address God not only as Creator and Master, but also as Father. Jesus

Christ said that we should do this. 'When you pray', He told the apostles, say 'our Father, who art in Heaven . . .' How is this possible?

Remember that in baptism, God places His Holy Spirit within us. But when He does this, He's giving us a share in His own nature. God is so powerful that He's able to share His own nature even with weak creatures such as ourselves.

Now when I speak of God 'sharing His nature', you mustn't imagine that He Himself would then have 'less' of His own nature, like someone sharing a cake. Think instead of a teacher who shares his knowledge with a pupil, without losing any of it himself. That's an image of what God does. He shares with us His own blessedness, that's to say, His knowledge and love of Himself. After all, if even good men desire to share their happiness with others, how much more God, who is goodness itself!

So after we're baptized, we have 'something in common' with God. We have a participation in the divine nature, as the apostle St Peter says. That makes an entirely new relationship possible between ourselves and Him: friendship. We always remain infinitely beneath God, since He is our creator and we are His creatures. Yet there's also, we can dare to say, a kind of 'equality' between us, once He's clothed us with His own nature.

Doesn't the Koran describe Abraham as a 'friend of God' (Sura 4:125)? Now friendship always implies a certain equality. It's impossible for a man to have a friendship with a cat or a fish. We can't have any kind of equality with God by nature, for in comparison to Him we are nothing. But when He puts His grace into our souls and makes us resemble Him, then we can have a friendship with Him.

We have not only a 'needy love' for God, wanting to be with Him. We can even have a 'generous love' for God, being glad that He is so blessed in Himself.

That explains why we can call God 'our Father'. Once God has shared His divinity with us, we resemble Him somewhat as a son resembles his human father. This doesn't detract from His greatness. On the contrary, it's a proof of His greatness, that He can take even mortal men and make them His children, modelled on Jesus Christ, His eternal Son. That's how we come to love God as He loves us, and address Him reverently but with confidence as 'Father'.

But finally, what of your objection that a father is grieved when his children suffer harm or turn out badly, and that this can't be true of God? But of course when we use the same word of God and of some human being, we don't mean that *everything* that's true of the man is also true of God. For example, when we call a man wise, we mean that he's studied hard and learned many things, and that he thinks carefully before undertaking some important venture. But when we call God 'wise', we don't mean any of these things. We simply mean that He knows all there is to know.

It's the same with the word 'Father'. When we call God our Father we don't mean that He will be literally disappointed if we turn out badly (even though the Bible does talk by a metaphor of God being grieved by men's sins). No, we mean first of all that His love for His creatures is real and generous; and secondly that of His own free will He 'begets' Christians to share in His nature and to live 'for the praise of His glory'.

With best wishes,

Christophorus

Letter Fourteen

ON LOVE FOR OUR ENEMIES

Dear Ali,

You say that you understand better now what's meant by the love of God, but that you still want to know more about our teaching on love. 'Jesus Christ said that we should love our enemies, and that if someone strikes us on the right side of the face we should offer the other side as well. But surely this is unnecessary, and a sign of weakness. Someone who respects himself will stand up for his rights and not let others walk all over him. What if everyone in a country did what Christ says – it would certainly be conquered by its neighbours!'

Remember what I said last time, that by baptism we receive a share in God's nature. This means that our actions can resemble God's. Now, how does God treat His enemies? (By His 'enemies', I means those who make themselves His enemies: those who don't love Him and refuse to accept His will.) The Gospel tells us: 'He makes his sun to rise upon the good and the bad, and he sends rain upon the just and the unjust.' In other words, He continues to give good things even to those who rebel against Him and defy Him. But this is a sign of love, since to love someone means to will that they should have what is good. In other words, God Himself, whom

Christians imitate, loves His enemies.

It's not just natural good things, either, like the sun and the rain, that God sends to those who don't love Him. He also gives them what is much better, the chance to repent. Through His prophet Ezekiel He said, 'As I live, I desire not the death of the wicked man but rather that He should turn from his sin and live.' Best of all, He sent His only Son to die for us not because we were already good, but 'when we were still sinners', as St Paul says.

So God loves His enemies. This isn't because He's weak, as if He were afraid that they might hurt Him! God loves His enemies because He is goodness itself, and it's the very nature of goodness to grant good things to others. Certainly, He is also just, and if men remain defiant and proud to the very end they won't share God's happiness after death. But even then, they won't be totally excluded from God's generosity. They'll still owe their existence to Him, as I said last time. Meanwhile, God desires all men, even great sinners, to convert and be saved.

So this is the model for us to follow. When Christ said, 'Love your enemies, do good to them that hate you', He added this reason why: '. . . and you shall be the sons of the Most High, for he is kind to the unthankful and the evil.' When we love our enemies we resemble God and become more fit to be called His 'sons'.

Jesus Himself set us an example of this. He prayed for those who were crucifying Him, saying, 'Father, forgive them, for they know not what they do.' St Stephen, the first disciple to be martyred, said of those who were stoning him to death, 'Lord, lay not this sin to their charge.' In fact, all those whom we reckon as martyrs died praying for their enemies. This is the proof that they were dying out of love for God, not from pride or hatred or some other reason.

Now, none of this means that we can never use force against anyone. Catholics aren't pacifists. Jesus Christ was not a pacifist; in fact, one of the people whom He praised most highly was a Roman centurion. Loving our enemies simply means that we must never *hate* anyone. We must never desire that anyone should go to hell, for example. Even when a soldier is fighting in a war, he shouldn't hate those he's fighting. If he kills anyone, he should pray for that man's soul.

We say that the State has authority to take life for two reasons. It can take life in a just war. This means a war that is fought for a just cause, and in which non-combatants are never deliberately attacked. The State may also execute wrong-doers, if they've been guilty of a very grave crime. A private individual, on the other hand, may never set out to kill anyone; but if he's attacked, he can resist his assailant with as much force as is necessary to save his own life. If the only way to do this is to kill the other person, then he is blameless. But in all these cases there must be no hatred for the one who has made himself our enemy. The law of Christ forbids us to take pleasure in his suffering as such. And however much harm someone may have done to us or to our family, we must forgive that person, at least to the extent of desiring his repentance. If he was starving or seriously wounded, and there was no one else to help him, God would expect us to go to his aid.

It's true that Christ said some things that might sound as if we could never use any kind of force. But not everything which He said was meant to apply in a literal sense to everyone. In that passage about turning the other cheek, for example, He was inculcating an attitude of the soul. We should have such patience and humility that *we should be ready* to offer no resistance to an assailant: unless we had some duty to resist. But sometimes there is a duty to resist. For example, a father has to protect his family, and a king or a president must protect his country. Yet even when a householder fights off someone who would attack his children, or a general fights off an invader, they mustn't let their inner attitude be one of murderous hatred.

But if someone doesn't have a duty to resist, then he may be able to fulfil Christ's sayings about non-resistance more literally. For example, He once said, 'If a man would take away from you your tunic, do not forbid him to take your cloak also.' This means that we should be so free from avarice as to lose our possessions without a murmur. But it reminds me of the story of St John Kanty, a Polish priest. He was set upon one day by highwaymen, who demanded his money with threats. St John handed it over, naturally; but when they had gone off again, he remembered that he had some gold coins sewn into his clothes for safe-keeping. He realized that he'd accidentally told them an untruth, by saying that he'd handed over all his money when he hadn't; so he ran after them and explained that he had some gold coins which they'd better take as well (by the way, the robbers were so amazed at his goodness that they gave everything back).

However, I don't think that John Kanty would have done that if he'd been a married man. It would have been his duty to keep hold of those gold coins to help support his family. But since he was a priest, and therefore celibate, he could give them up. One can renounce one's own rights, but not other people's. Yet even if he had been married and unable to put Christ's words into practice literally, he could still have kept them in spirit. He could at least have been willing to have handed over the gold coins, if he could have done so without harming anyone else.

So do you still think that it's a sign of weakness to love one's enemies? Surely, anything that makes us more like God must be a sign of strength. After all, the man who hates his enemies is just yielding to a natural inclination, and that doesn't take any particular strength of character. A dog or a cat reacts with fury when another animal takes away its food, and when we hate someone who harms us, we're acting rather like that. It's the man who can rise above insults, and act towards his enemies as God acts towards *His*, who is truly strong. To keep one's heart free of hatred, to pray for the conversion of one who has done us evil, all the while resisting him if necessary for our own safety or for the good of those entrusted to our care; that is an attitude worthy of a man, and of a child of God.

With best wishes,
Christophorus

Letter Fifteen

ON THE SOUL

Dear Ali,

You say that you still need time to reflect on the doctrines of Christianity that you've heard about so far, but that in the meantime you'd like to know what I think about some philosophical problems. First of all you want to discuss the soul, which I mentioned a couple of letters ago. Let me quote your own words: 'Doesn't the idea of the soul belong to a pre-scientific age? After all, scientists discover more and more about human beings, and how they work, and they never have recourse to the soul in any of their explanations. Or if by the soul we just mean that human beings can think and make choices, can't the other animals do that, though in a more rudimentary way? Is it really possible to prove that there is something immortal in men – something that will survive the death of our bodies? I wish I could be sure.'

Let's begin by defining the soul. What's the difference between a living man, and the same man a moment after his death? As long as he's alive, he is *one thing*, a single substance. When he's died he's no longer one single substance; his body isn't unified as it was before. In the living body, the parts work together for the sake of the whole. In the corpse, the parts are no longer bound together; they go their own way, and so the body decomposes.

This means there is *something* in the living body which is not in the corpse. It's not the brain, the liver, the heart, nor any of the other organs, nor is it the flesh or the bone. These all remain in the corpse, at least for a time. No: it's something that makes these disparate parts into one unified thing. And this 'principle of unity', which exists in the body until the moment of death but not afterwards, is what I mean by the 'soul'.

You might object: in that case not only human beings have souls, but every other living thing! For all of them have a unity in themselves until the moment of death, but not afterwards.

Well, at the risk of surprising you, I should agree: each living thing does have a soul, for else it wouldn't be *one* thing. But that's not to say that all living things enjoy some form of life after death. There are souls and souls: only human beings have immortal souls. The souls of plants and animals don't survive the death of the plant or animal, for a reason I'll give later on.

But if you find it too incongruous to talk about the soul of a spider or an oak-tree, I'm perfectly happy to find some other word. Definitions are free, after all. Why don't we restrict the term 'soul' to human beings, and use some other phrase for the other creatures, such as 'principle of life and unity'? (A little cumbersome, I'm afraid: perhaps after all it's best to stay with 'soul'.)

You'll see now why biologists and physiologists never have recourse to the notion of the soul in all the admirable explanations that they give us of the working of the human body. It's because, whether they know it or not, the soul is *presupposed* in all they say. So they can tell us, for example, how electrical impulses pass from the brain to the hand in some reflex action, or how acids in the stomach help to digest what has been eaten, and no matter how detailed their explanations become, they never have to invoke the soul as a factor. Yet all the time they are *presuming*, as is only natural, that the body is alive and unified; in other words, that it has a soul. So the soul, precisely because it is the necessary presupposition of these disciplines, can never be one of their objects of investigation, rather as a fighter pilot who scrutinizes enemy territory, doesn't scrutinize but simply presupposes the laws of aerodynamics which enable him to fly.

But now, what of my claim that human beings, unlike spiders or oak-trees, have immortal souls? You might argue that to judge from what I've said so far, an immortal soul is a contradiction in terms. I've said that a soul is the principle of unity of a living body; but when death occurs, there is no more unity – so doesn't it follow that there is no more soul?

That's going rather too quickly (somebody once said, 'Philosophers should greet each other with the words, "Take it slowly"'). If the soul were *only* a principle of the body's unity, then it wouldn't survive death, but of course it may be other things as well. Let's consider one of man's primary characteristics, namely the ability to think. Now I don't agree, as you suggested in your letter – though perhaps you were only playing the devil's advocate – that other animals have a capacity to think which differs from ours only in degree. Take an animal that seems quite 'intelligent', such as a cat. When he's standing by an open front door, looking out, and swinging his tail, but otherwise motionless, we might say, 'He's wondering whether or not to go outside.' But even as we say it, we're conscious of something mildly humorous in our words, of talking about the cat as if it were human. For no one seriously supposes that the cat is saying to itself, only too quietly to be heard, or even thinking to itself, 'If I go out, then I'll have the opportunity to prowl around the bottom of that tree with the fledgling birds that I discovered yesterday, but on the other hand there may be no one to let me back into the house when the time comes for my nap.' It may be that the twin instincts of hunting birds and fear of losing comfort are at work in the cat, and that its apparent 'indecision' comes from this, that for a while neither predominates. But no one seriously supposes that a cat conceptualises its instincts, speaking to itself in the way that I imagined.

Human beings, however, have precisely this power of forming concepts, which is what enables us to speak. For example, from seeing birds, we form the concept of 'bird', and designate it with a word. A cat can't do this: it can see individual birds, and perhaps retain images of particular birds that it has seen, images that may later prompt it to hunt in certain locations: but it can't form an abstract concept of 'bird' as such, nor say to itself, 'I like hunting birds.' Only man can contemplate an object which is *universal*, and think about birds as such, as opposed to just seeing or remembering this or that particular bird.

We human beings, then, can have 'universals' existing in our minds: objects which have been stripped of their individuality. Yet none of the things that we see or hear or touch is of this kind: we never see 'bird' as such or 'whiteness' as such, but only this or that bird, and this or that example of whiteness. So how do the individual things that we sense yield up the universal 'meaning' which the senses can't reach, but the intellect can? Well, what is it that makes the things individual in the first place? What is it, for example, that makes this blackbird sitting on my window-sill to be different from this other blackbird in the tree? Is it simply the fact that they exist in different places? No, since they have first to be different in order to exist in different places. Then what is it that differentiates one physical thing from another of the same species? Isn't it simply that their bodies are made of different portions of matter? At any rate, as soon as something is material, it can't help but be an individual, separated from all other beings in creation. The matter 'seals it off' from all other things. For as long as it remains where it is, it can never be anywhere else.

A 'universal', on the other hand, is just something which can exist in more than one place. It's not limited or constricted. When I see a bird on the lawn I am contemplating something that exists there and nowhere else; when I *think*, 'bird', I am contemplating something that exists in many places at once. But this means that the thing in my mind is *free of matter*. If it had matter in it, it would no longer be a universal object; it would inevitably be something singular, like the bird on the lawn.

In other words, when we abstract some concept from the things we see around us, our object of thought is raised up from the material state in which it exists in the outside world, so as to exist for thought in an immaterial way. All the universal objects of our thought, bird, green, justice, are as such *immaterial* – otherwise, they wouldn't be universal.

But what follows from this? If the object of our thought is something non-material, our thinking must also be non-material. No material action can bear on something non-material; there's no way in which it could come into contact with it. So the action of thinking, bearing as it does on immaterial objects, must itself be immaterial.

But this means that our intellect, that by which we think, must also be non-material. No material thing can produce a non-material activity, which thinking is. If something is wholly material then its actions are the actions of matter. But since our intellect is capable of non-material action, it too must be non-material. Or to put it another way, our intellect is spiritual, for spiritual simply means 'that which has no matter in it'.

I haven't quite finished answering your questions, but I think that's enough for one letter. I'll take up the threads again next time I write.

With best wishes,

Christophorus

Letter Sixteen

ON LIFE AFTER DEATH

Dear Ali,

You may be wondering why I went into such detail in my last letter about the nature of human knowledge. The point of it was to show you that we have at least one non-material power within us, namely our intellect. The reason this matters is that if something is non-material, then it's not destroyed by death. For death is the separation of our body into its individual material constituents: but our intellect has *no* material constituents. It can't decay or decompose, as material organs do. In other words, there's something in each of us that survives bodily death. The lower animals, on the other hand, can't think or reason; they're confined to what they can sense. They can know individual material things, but they don't have universal ideas. All their activities and faculties are material, and so nothing in them survives death.

But should we talk only about our intellects surviving after death, and not about our souls? No. Whatever it is that unifies our bodily parts and functions, and which in my last letter I called the soul, also unifies our bodily actions with our mental ones. What I mean is this: everyone is conscious that all his actions, whether bodily or mental, walking, laughing, praying, thinking or anything else, are actions of *one* subject. It is *I* who do all these things, not just parts of me. The same subject can both think of an abstruse mathematical problem and also get into a fight. Our intellect, in other words, is subject to that same principle of unity that unifies all our bodily functions and activities. Our intellect is subject to our soul; technically, it's called a 'faculty of the soul'.

But we've just seen that our intellect is spiritual and that it therefore survives death. It follows that our soul must do the same. The soul couldn't have a spiritual faculty unless it were spiritual itself. Or to put it another way, our soul is the root principle of all our actions including the activity of thinking. Our soul, then, produces at least one action which is independent of matter; it follows that it doesn't depend on matter for its being. For nothing can act independently of matter except what can exist independently of matter: as our philosophers say, 'activity follows being'. Only what is spiritual can act spiritually. Therefore the human soul, unlike all other souls, can and does survive death.

But what exactly happens to the soul after death? The soul is parted from the body: that's the very definition of human death. But where does it go? As you know, some people have suggested that all souls flow together into one great soul, or into God, like rivulets flowing into the sea. But that isn't just against the Catholic faith, it's against sound philosophy. We human beings find it difficult to conceive something truly spiritual without letting our imaginations intervene too much. But as soon as we start to think clearly, it's obvious that human souls can't flow into each other so as to lose their own identity, precisely because they *are* spiritual and not material. To flow together means that the parts of one thing and the parts of another are so interspersed that the two can no longer be distinguished. But a soul doesn't have parts in that way; it's not a very rarefied gas. If you wanted to have a mental image, it'd be truer to imagine a soul as a point in space. Not that that's a particularly good image, but at least it helps remind us that no soul can 'flow into' or 'be lost in' another soul, or the universe or the 'World-Soul' (whatever that's supposed to be).

Least of all, of course, can a soul 'flow into God' so as to lose its own independent being. If that could happen it would mean that God was changeable, and could be 'increased' by creatures. But then, of course, he wouldn't be God at all.

What about reincarnation? Can a soul go back into some other body, or even into some non-human creature? I suppose that it's theoretically possible, in the sense of not a contradiction in terms, that God could send a human soul that has left a body back to a new embryo who's just come into being. Yet to do that would be contrary to God's wisdom. For the soul, remember, is only a part of the human being. Our body isn't simply a garment that we wear, it's part of us: if you strike my body, you strike *me*. The soul is the more important part of the person, granted, but the whole person is the soul and body together. So if God caused my soul to exist in some other body, it would be some other person who would come into being.

But in that case God would be taking more care of a part than of the whole; He'd be treating my soul as if it were more important than my person. He'd be acting as if it didn't matter what person was constituted by my soul, so long as my soul existed in some body or another. whereas in fact the soul exists for the sake of the person, as a part always exists for the sake of the whole. So the Church holds that God will send all souls back into bodies, but each into its own body, at the end of time. This is what we call the general resurrection, when the souls that have remained separated from their bodies will be re-united to them, and so the same persons will be constituted as before. Not that we hold the doctrine of the resurrection on philosophical grounds, since it's an article of faith; but we call philosophy in support of the faith.

But, you ask, 'what are departed souls doing between death and the final resurrection? Are they doing anything at all, or are they simply sleeping?' Some people have thought that human souls remain in a sort of unconscious state until the whole person rises again at the end of time: but this isn't the Catholic faith. We say that the soul is in one of three places, heaven, hell or purgatory. And wherever it is, it's not unconscious: after all, the soul is the very thing that made the man conscious during his life on earth, causing his body to be more than just inert matter. So it's not reasonable to suppose that when the soul has departed it suddenly becomes inert itself.

As I tried to show last time, our thinking, and therefore our loving or hating, depends on our being free from matter to some extent. But after death the soul is much more free from matter than it was before. So after death the soul, wherever it is, will live much more intensely than the man did on earth. The dead are more alive than we are: for good or ill.

You may know that we believe in a judgment after

death, as well as at the end of time. The apostle St Paul says, 'It is appointed unto man once to die, and after that the judgment.' And that corresponds to another condition of the soul after death, namely its *immutability*. I don't mean that souls after death are absolutely unchanging. Only God is completely unchangeable. But departed souls are unchanging in one very important respect: they can no longer alter their *ultimate end*, the thing that they love above all else. You see, God has made our souls in such a way that they come by means of the body to decide what their ultimate end will be. For example, during their earthly life some people see the creation and by means of it come to know and love God above all else. Other people see the same creation, but make it the means for pursuing their own private ambitions and pleasures, loving themselves best of all. But each group of people *sets their soul in a certain direction* by using what they have learned through their bodily senses: that is how human beings 'work'. When the body falls away, at death, the soul remains perpetually set in the direction that it had given to itself by the end of its earthly life. For eternity, it loves either God or itself above all else. As it says in our Scriptures, 'As the tree falls, whether to the south or to the north, there shall it lie.'

With best wishes,

Christophorus

ON FREE WILL

Dear Ali,

You say you'd like to hear more about the situation of souls after death, but that you've another question that's even more urgent. Judgment after death, you rightly say, presupposes that we were free on earth. We can't be rewarded for having done good or punished for having committed evil unless we were free to choose our actions. But you write: 'I feel that I'm free, but I don't see how I can be, for two reasons. First of all, if I do something, that must be because I desire to do it. But then the desire that I feel seems to be the explanation of my action; and so my action seems to be caused inevitably by a preceding desire, just as a billiard ball is inevitably moved when another strikes it. But if my action is inevitable, then it's not free! Secondly, we must surely believe that everything comes about as God wills. But then my good and bad actions must come about as God wills, and I wasn't really free to avoid then, even if it felt to me as though I was. Or if I really was free, how could God know in advance whether I should choose a good action or a bad one? Does He have to wait and see?'

I think you're wise to begin by saying, 'I feel I am free'. There are some things that we know in our hearts even before we can prove them; and we need to hold on to them when our philosophical reasonings tie us up in knots. Still, the truth of the heart can never contradict the truth of reason, so let's try to unravel these knotty questions.

I agree that our free choices must have some cause, or else they could never come into being. Materialists, of course, people who don't accept the existence of anything beyond what their senses report, suppose that a 'free' choice is an event in the brain caused by other physical events, and so ultimately that it's not free at all. But apart from the fact that it's plainly ridiculous to say that a choice, for example, to fight for one's country is *really* a movement of electrical charges in the brain – it would be like saying that the number 5 was *really* a fish, or that love is *really* made of cardboard – we've already seen that materialism is false. Our intellect is spiritual; if it weren't, it wouldn't be able to conceive of ideals above matter, such as truth and justice. And our will must also be spiritual, or else it wouldn't be able to seek to put such ideals into practice.

But I don't agree that our desires are the causes of our actions in quite the way that you suggest. It's a simple fact of experience that we can desire to do something, even desire it very much, and yet not do it, perhaps because we consider that our duty lies in the opposite direction. Of course you might respond: 'Then we are following the desire to do our duty, which proves in this instance to be stronger than the other'. But I wonder, is this really true? A man may have no *desire* in the normal sense of that word, to do his duty; no feeling of attraction towards it, or pleasurable anticipation of having done it; and yet do it all the same. Or if it's true in a sense that we only perform those actions that we desire to, 'desire' here simply refers to *the free choice itself* to act in a certain way. But what causes this free choice in the first place? It needn't be any kind of preceding desire; and even when such a desire is present, this doesn't make the choice inevitable, or otherwise how would vehement desires ever be resisted when weaker ones are sometimes followed?

I think that your picture of a desire clashing against the will like one billiard ball running into another and knocking it in an inevitable direction is a wrong one. Desires do influence our free choices, but more like citizens lobbying a Member of Parliament to vote in a certain way, than like one billiard ball cannoning into another. Then what does cause my free choices? The simplest answer is, 'I do'. Just as an MP listens to the opinions of his constituents and then makes up his own mind how to vote, so we're solicited by desires of various kinds, but choose for ourselves which if any to follow. If we are dutiful, we follow those desires that serve the ends for which God made us; if not, we follow those which accord with our private ambitions, or simply those that are most pressing.

But, you may say, surely I can't be the first and ultimate cause of my own choices, since that would make me an 'uncaused cause', which is one of the definitions of God. I agree: even though there's nothing *in creation* apart from ourselves which causes our choices, still we can't choose, just as we can't do anything at all, except under the influence of God. Everything 'real' in our choices and actions, all their physical and spiritual energy, comes from God, 'in whom we live and move and have our being'.

But now, have I answered your first objection only to fall into your second? If God moves us to act, doesn't this take away our free will? And since we sometimes go wrong, doesn't this explanation make God the author of sin? Here we've reached the question that has given philosophers and theologians more headaches than perhaps any other, so let's take things especially slowly.

Since God is goodness itself, He moves all creatures to act well. But He moves all things to act according to their own nature. For example, since plants have no powers of knowledge of any kind, God causes them to take in nourishment by purely physical processes, such as osmosis. Animals, on the other hand, have sense-knowledge, and so God causes them to direct themselves to their food by virtue of what they've seen or heard or smelled.

Now when God moves human beings to act, He takes into account two important features of our nature, namely that we're *free* and that we're *fallible*. We're free because none of our desires for particular things can compel our consent: the only thing that could infallibly make us choose it would be goodness itself, that's to say, God Himself, seen face-to-face. We're also fallible, by which I mean not just that we can make mistakes in our judgments, but that we can choose things that merely seem good in preference to truly good things, *even when we know them to be not truly worthy*: for example, a married man who has an illicit affair.

So God always moves us to make good choices, but He does so in a way that never takes away our freedom, and which doesn't usually take away our fallibility (He can cause us by a special grace to do some good action infallibly, but that's not His normal way of guiding us). God doesn't take away our freedom; on the contrary He *gives* us our freedom. He moves us not just to choose a thing, but to choose it freely. For when God moves our will, He moves it to act in accordance with its own nature, and it's the very nature of the will to choose freely, without being drawn irresistibly by any particular object.

But neither does He take away our fallibility. Even though we can't will any good unless we're moved by God, there is one thing that we can do without God, namely *to resist Him*. Imagine that God is moving us to choose some good action, for example to tell the truth because it's our duty, even though it would be less painful and embarrassing to tell a lie. If we don't resist God, then we shall choose to tell the truth. Our good choice will be God's gift to us, yet it will also be a product of our own freedom. We shall have been moved by Him towards freely telling the truth.

But if we do resist God and, so to speak, 'fall away' from His guidance, what happens? Our will is no longer guided by God, and so it falls under the dominion of some private desire of our own, in this case a desire to avoid pain or embarrassment. Then when God moves us to choose our action, we choose to tell a lie. This choice, *considered as a reality in our will*, is from God; but considered as a sin, as something that conflicts with God's law, it's caused by our falling away from God's guidance. So God is still working in us even when we make a bad choice, for unless He were, we couldn't choose at all; yet the *badness* of our choice – the discrepancy between it and God's law – springs from us and not from Him.

So we can do nothing good without God; yet by our own initiative we can introduce evil into the world. As it says in our Scriptures, 'God made man from the beginning and left him in the hand of his own counsel.'

'But isn't God's will always fulfilled', you ask? Yes: in one way or another. Either a human being doesn't resist God's guidance, and then His will is fulfilled in a straightforward manner; or else he does resist, and then God's will is fulfilled which decrees that even those who fall away from His good guidance will still receive the power to choose an action of some kind. Their choice of action, of course, will be marked by selfishness. Yet even though this evil is contrary to God's will, He wills to allow it to enter creation when a creature resists His guidance. In other words, nothing happens in the world except what God wills directly or else wills to permit.

But more than this, God can never be defeated. Whatever His creatures may do against Him, He will always draw some good out of it. And the good which is drawn from the evil will be greater, in the end, than the good which was excluded by the evil in the first place. So the sin of our first parents excluded something which would certainly have been very good – the transmission of their grace and happiness to their children. But God brought about something even better in response to this sin: His incarnation as Man, and the infinite merits of Christ's life and death, and all the saints ransomed by His precious Blood.

You ask, how can God know in advance whether I will do right or wrong? But of course, God doesn't know anything 'in advance'. Being eternal, He doesn't have to wait for the future or remember the past. He is *above* time; the day of Creation, and your reading this letter, and the day of Judgment, are all things present to Him that He sees now. So whether we act well or badly, whether God's will is done in us straightforwardly or only after we have tried to thwart it, He sees this from all eternity. He sees it in the Light in which He sees all things, His own self.

With best wishes,

Christophorus

Letter Eighteen

ON EVIL AND SUFFERING

Dear Ali,

My remarks on free-will have set you thinking about the question of evil. As you say, the word 'evil' seems to be used in two different senses. We talk, first, of evil deeds. Evil here means 'moral evil': something opposed to virtue and God's law. But we also talk about 'the evils in the world', meaning things like sickness and famine, or more generally, suffering. These things are certainly bad, but not bad in quite the same way as, say, murder. They're what we call 'natural evils'. And you want to know what Christians say about the relation between these two sorts of evil. Is suffering always caused by some previous sin? You write, 'I feel sure there must be a connexion, yet it often seems to be the innocent who suffer more than the guilty.' And you want to know how to answer your Hindu friend who says that the suffering of an innocent child proves his doctrine of reincarnation. If a child is suffering, he says, then since Reality is ultimately just, he must have committed crimes in a previous life, which he is now expiating.

This is a question where we have to pick our way carefully. God's will is simple, yet when it touches our fallen world it often seems complex, like light falling onto a shattered mirror. So in the first place, the instinct of your heart is once more correct, according to the Catholic faith. Suffering has *something* to do with sin. Remember what we believe about the creation of man and his fall. Our first parents were at peace with God and with each other for as long as they placed His will above all else; and a special gift of God preserved them from the threat of sickness or bodily death. But as soon as they committed that first sin, they began to suffer. They suffered from feeling themselves at odds with God and from shame at what they'd done. But they also lost the gift by which their bodies were preserved from sickness, death and decay.

Suffering entered the world because of sin. And since that first sin affects all later generations, it's a partial explanation of the suffering in the world today. For example, if a baby is suffering from some sickness, we can say that this is a result of original sin, which took away our immunity to the ills that threaten human nature. Be careful here: I don't say that the baby is *punished* on account of Adam's sin. No one can be justly punished for another's crime. But the baby is still suffering because of that sin, in the sense that he wouldn't be suffering if it hadn't been committed. We could even say that *human nature*, which fell in Adam, is suffering there on account of its own sin – though we mustn't say that of the child itself.

So original sin is at the root of the suffering in the world. But you want to know whether suffering can also be explained by the sins that people commit here and now. It's obvious that great sins do frequently bring suffering to other people, for example when a dictator's greed brings famine upon his land. But does God ever punish people in this life on account of their *own* sins? Here again we have to be careful. Yes, men's sufferings can be a punishment sent from God for their sins, but they aren't necessarily so. So we should never say or think, 'Such and such a person is suffering on account of his sins.' We can't know, without a special revelation from God, why a particular person is suffering, and we should make it our habit to assume the best about others (on the other hand, if *we* are suffering something, it's a good practice to offer our pains to God, to help make up for the times when we know we have offended Him).

You ask me, 'what purpose can suffering serve, if it's not a punishment for sins? Why does an all-wise Providence allow it?' We can give several answers to that question, though, as I say, without a special revelation we can't know which the true explanation is in any given case.

First of all, then, God can use suffering to make a good man better. When his earthly supports give way, a good man will turn in a more heartfelt way to the 'strong, living God'. I think this was true of Tobias in the Old Testament. When he went blind, he began to pray even more fervently than in the days of his sight. St Paul says that God disciplines *all* His faithful children in some such way.

Again, God may allow a good man to suffer for the sake of others. We can be inspired when we see how nobly one of God's servants bears with affliction out of love for God. There's a whole book of the Bible, the Book of Job, that gives us a picture of suffering heroically borne (though Job wasn't absolutely without fault in the way he spoke about his sufferings, so true is it that even the best of men are fallen). What's more, according to our faith, such a man doesn't just *inspire* others; by offering his pains to God, he can make reparation for their sins. He can imitate Christ, who saved the world by the Cross.

Sometimes God allows a person to suffer something not because of some wrong that he's already done, but to prevent him from committing some wrong. For example, God may see that if a man goes to a certain place in company with certain people, he will fall into sin. If He sends him a sickness to prevent him travelling on that day, He won't be punishing the man, but having mercy on him.

Or again, God may allow someone to suffer as a way of punishing some *other* person. This is what happened to King David, when his little son died as a result of the king's adulterous affair with Bathsheba. The child wasn't punished for his father's sin: the father was punished and corrected by his son's death. I suppose someone might ask, 'was this fair on the son?' But remember that human nature has no *right* to be protected against the ills that threaten it; and I should think that God had some way of compensating the child, after death, for his short life on earth.

We also know from revelation that God permits some ills simply in order to put them right, so that men may believe. When the apostles asked of a certain blind man whether he or his parents had sinned, that he should have been born blind, Jesus Christ replied: 'Neither has this man sinned, nor his parents: but that the works of God should be made manifest in him.' He then gave the man his sight, as a result of which some of the leading

Jews believed in Him.

Perhaps some of these reasons show why it may be, as you suggest, that the innocent can suffer more than the guilty, or to be more precise, as we are all sinners, why those who are seeking to do God's will may suffer more than those who have no thought of God. Only a good man will grow in virtue by means of suffering or be able to set an example to others by his patient endurance; a hard-hearted or unbelieving man will generally be made worse by suffering, and since God has a love even for people of this kind, He doesn't want to send them what will make them worse. Likewise only a good man will be able to imitate Christ and offer up his own sufferings for the sins of others.

A great pope once said that when a sick man has a chance of recovery, his physician won't spare him, but will administer even bitter medicines and painful operations whilst there's still a chance of his cure; but that if the patient's condition becomes hopeless, his physician will let him indulge his every whim, and eat and drink whatever he wants. So it is, said Pope Gregory, with the human race and God. As long as we're capable of amendment, God will allow trials to amend us, through His grace; but if we become incurable, He may let us have our own way, in this life.

That suggests still another reason why better men may suffer more than others. God doesn't want all our thoughts to be absorbed by this present life. So when we see that justice isn't done on this earth, but that guilty men sometimes flourish while their victims receive no redress, we spontaneously say, 'There must be another life!' In this way God doesn't allow the human race to forget completely about judgment and the world to come. 'God sees to it that men fear Him', says the Book of Ecclesiastes. And He also sees to it that they hope in Him.

Yet is it, after all, quite true that better men suffer more? In some ways it may be; perhaps in health, or in worldly possessions; or perhaps they are more aware than others how they have failed to use God's gifts well. But the deepest suffering comes from having a mind at enmity with its maker. So another of our saints has said: 'The disordered soul is its own punishment'. Likewise, the deepest happiness is to love God and to know that no creature, however powerful, can separate us from His love. And this is the happiness of all good men.

With best wishes,
Christophorus

Letter Nineteen

ON THE NEED
FOR THE CHURCH

Dear Ali,

You want to take up an offer that I made in the first of these letters, to explain to you the difference between Catholics and other groups that are called 'Christian'. 'Isn't the main thing', you say, 'to live as a child of God, worshipping Him in faith, hope and love? I can see why Christians would want to band together to encourage each other in their lives as children of God. But why should anyone insist on a need to belong to this group of Christians rather than another?'

Let me congratulate you, if I may, on your succinct summary of the Christian life: 'to live as a child of God, worshipping Him in faith, hope and love'. Yes, we believe that this is why we were put on earth. But the question arises, how *do* we worship God in faith, hope and love? Is it enough just to compose prayers, or to find prayers in the Bible, and to pray them to God, alone or with others, with as much faith, hope and love as we can muster? That's certainly an excellent thing to do, and I should be glad if all men did it; but is it the best way to worship God? What if He desires something more? How can we know?

Again, 'faith' means believing whatever God tells us. But what *has* God told us? If you investigate the different groups called 'Christian', you'll see that they don't agree on this most important question.

How then can we be confident that we're living as God intends, believing all that He's revealed and worshipping Him in the way He desires? We can't: unless there are men on earth with the authority to teach us in Christ's name.

Notice that I say *men*, rather than 'a book'. We do of course have a book which we say is inspired by God: our holy Bible. Yet no book by itself, not even an inspired one, can take the place of a living teacher. For one thing, no book can correct those who understand it wrongly. As one of the old philosophers said, books are read by wise men and ignorant ones alike, and they can't defend themselves when men mistake their meaning.

What's more, important questions have arisen and still arise which aren't dealt with in the Bible. For example: Should little children be baptized? What's the proper day of the week for Christians to worship? What lawful means may infertile couples use to bring about conception? These are serious questions, to which sure answers must be provided.

Don't think that I'm lacking esteem for our Holy Scriptures, when I say that we need something more! We hold that every sentence in the Scriptures was inspired by the Holy Spirit; they've given us the best portrait of Jesus Christ that human words ever will; they're a never-failing source of light and comfort for those who read them with faith. But they weren't meant to be a 'self-help guide', to solve all our questions without recourse to any other human being.

Consider what's happened over the last 500 years. I'm sure you've learned about the movement called 'Protestantism', which arose in the sixteenth century. Protestantism holds that a man can know all the truth he needs simply by reading his bible in a prayerful way. But those who've followed this path are today divided among themselves into innumerable groups, disagreeing with each other about many and grave questions. Where there's no Church with authority to teach what God has revealed, then everyone frames a Christianity for himself. We've reached the point today, outside the Catholic Church, where there's *no* doctrine of the faith which isn't denied by someone or other who calls himself a Christian, no, not even the very existence of God Himself.

But Christ came to deliver us from the tyranny of self-will. So he left behind Him, Catholics hold, a body of men who have the authority to teach in His Name. These were the twelve apostles, chosen personally by Jesus to be the 'light of the world'. Before they died, they appointed successors, called bishops, and these in turn appointed other bishops to succeed them. And the Catholic Church is composed of all those people who've been baptized and who acknowledge the authority of these bishops to teach the faith and to govern the Church. The bishops themselves are kept together because all must be in communion with the successor of St Peter, the Bishop of Rome, also called the Pope. If one of them ever repudiated the pope's authority, he'd no longer be a Catholic bishop.

So let's suppose that a question arises concerning our

faith – for example, does Scripture teach that Christ is truly God, or just that he is very like God, a very exalted creature, halfway between God and man? No one can claim that this is a trivial question. It decides the very essence of Christianity. Now I'm sure the Bible teaches that Christ is truly God: yet it would be possible for someone, if he was so minded, to dispute the passages that I should quote and to put forward others which might seem to support the opposite contention. So must we wrangle endlessly on so important a question? No, not if we are Catholics. At a certain point in history, the bishops assembled and solemnly pronounced judgment: Christ is true God, of one and the same nature with God the Father. This happened at the Council of Nicaea in the year 325. For a Catholic, that's the end of the matter. What has been once defined remains forever.

Or let's suppose that an advance in human knowledge gives rise to a new question of morality, as with the invention of the contraceptive pill. Is it lawful for a woman to make herself infertile for a time, so that she and her husband may enjoy the pleasure of marriage without the possibility of receiving a child from God? The Scriptures say much in praise of fruitfulness in marriage, but they don't answer this question directly. The great saints of the past who addressed similar questions seemingly say no: but someone may argue that they were condemning abortion rather than contraception; or that they were condemning unbridled passion more than contraception in itself and in all circumstances; or that even great saints are not infallible. And so a veil of confusion and uncertainty descends. Only a living authority, present on earth and for all to see and hear, can finally dispel these doubts. So in the year 1968 the Pope, in virtue of the authority that he holds from Christ, reiterated the teaching that it is wrong for a woman to make herself infertile so that she and her husband might enjoy the marital union without the possibility of children. For Catholics the question is answered; and married couples have a clear teaching, a teaching which may require strong faith to follow, but which gives them the comfort of knowing the will of Christ in this serious matter.

So I hope you're beginning to see why Catholics attach such importance to the Church. The Church isn't a sort of club for Christians, which we join simply to encourage one another to lead Christian lives. We join the Church to be taught by it; or rather, as we'd say, to be taught by her, since we think of the Church as our Mother, as I mentioned once before.

After all, consider what great lengths God went to in order to teach the human race its duties, according to our faith. He prepared a people for Himself over many centuries, raising up prophets and other inspired teachers, men like Noah, Abraham, Moses, David, Elijah, Isaiah, Malachi and many others. He gave them a law, and taught them in detail how to serve Him. Finally, out of His infinite goodness, He descended to His own creation and was born of the holy Virgin. He worked countless miracles on earth so that His people might believe, He accepted an agonizing death at their hands for the sins of the whole world; He rose again and ascended in glory, having sent out His chosen men and promised to be with them all days until the end of the world. Is it likely that having gone to such lengths to enlighten the human race, He would then abandon it to endless disputes, placing no living authority on earth for men to rely on, leaving every man, intelligent, average or slow, to his own judgment? I at any rate don't think so. As the Scriptures say, 'Wisdom reacheth from end to end mightily, and ordereth all things sweetly.'

With best wishes,

Christophorus

Letter Twenty

ON RECOGNIZING
THE TRUE CHURCH

Dear Ali,

You say that you see the need for what I've called a 'living authority' to decide disputed questions among Christians. Yet you're still puzzled that there should be quite so many divisions among those who profess to be believers in Christ. 'Was Christ's own teaching', you write, 'lacking in clarity? Didn't He at least make it clear what His Church would look like, so that Christians would be sure to belong to it?'

Our Lord's teaching, of course, in itself is clear. He once said, 'I speak that which I have seen with my Father'. There was no obscurity in His thoughts, since His human mind was, so to speak, bathed in the light of His divinity. Yet for various reasons He didn't always express His thoughts in such a way that His meaning would be immediately grasped by the average listener. In fact, to the crowds He always couched His teaching in 'parables', that's to say, similes and allegories. In part this was done so the weak would not be shocked by hearing something for which they weren't yet prepared. I mentioned before that Christ only gradually showed people who He was, so astonishing is that truth. In the same way, He only gradually showed people that the 'Kingdom' He'd come to found wouldn't be ruled by the sons of Israel, but be composed equally of men of all nations.

That's one reason why those who rely only on the words of Christ recorded in the four Gospels may not recognize the Catholic Church as the Kingdom that He founded. For He didn't say to the Jews, 'I'm going to found a new People of God which will supplant the sons of Israel; it will be governed from Rome, and most of its rulers will be of the stock of the Gentiles' – which would have been a clear description of the Catholic Church. If He had spoken like that, then most of the people would have been instantly alienated, and refused to listen to Him any more, to their own great loss. No, He had to lead His brethren gradually to the truth about the Church, since it was going to involve the surrender of one of their most cherished ideals, national glory. You can see from the 'Acts of the Apostles' that even after the Resurrection and the Ascension, the disciples took time to get used to the idea of equality between themselves and the Gentiles.

We can say something similar about many of the doctrines which separate Catholics from some of those who acknowledge Christ but aren't yet part of His visible Catholic Church. Our doctrines of the Holy Trinity and the Holy Eucharist, for example, were taught by Christ. But they weren't 'spelled out' by Him in quite the way that the Church, guided by His Holy Spirit, has since defined them. In part, as I say, this was because the Jewish mind needed time to assimilate these doctrines. You'll see in the Gospel of St John how even Christ's hints about the Holy Trinity and the Holy Eucharist led to uproar among the less spiritual of the Jews. But in part, I think, it was so that later generations of Christians might have the chance to learn humility through being taught by other human beings, rather than being able to say to the priests and bishops of the Church, 'I've got a Bible, I don't need you to teach me'.

Yet Jesus Christ foresaw, of course, that those who weren't brought up as children of His Catholic Church would need evidence that this was the Kingdom that He'd founded. So He said enough about His Church or Kingdom to enable them to recognize it. For one thing, He said that it would contain a great range of people, both saints and sinners. Many of His parables touch on this. He speaks of His Church as being like a net that contains both good and bad fish until it reaches the shore; as a banqueting hall where the good and the bad feast together; as a group of bridesmaids, half of whom are wise and half foolish. So in looking for the Church founded by Christ, we must look for one which has great saints, but we shouldn't expect it to be free of sinful men. I think that if you study history, you'll find that the Catholic Church, above all other bodies, has great numbers not only of virtuous members, but of men and women of outstanding holiness. She includes missionaries like St Francis Xavier who by his preaching converted tens of thousands of people in China and Japan; mystics like St Teresa of Avila, who's inspired thousands of young women to forego marriage and motherhood to devote themselves to a hidden life of prayer; priests like St John Bosco, whose example has led thousands of men to take vows of poverty, chastity and obedience, in order to educate children. Yet at the same time, the Catholic

Church doesn't reject those of her children who fall into sin. She encourages them to repent, but she doesn't cast them out of the Church. She remembers that Christ's net contains bad fish as well as good – and that the bad can become good before the net reaches the shore.

Another sign which Jesus said would mark out His Church is the presence of *miracles*. He said 'Signs', which means miracles, 'shall follow them that believe.' Very many of our saints have worked miracles, or rather, God has worked miracles through them. Read, for example, a life of Padre Pio, an Italian friar who died in 1968. He worked countless miracles. He once gave sight to a woman with no pupils in her eyes. Her case was famous throughout Italy: the doctors said that she oughtn't to be able to see! But very rarely if at all is it given to a non-Catholic to work a miracle, and never in defence of a doctrine which is contrary to the Catholic faith.

I think I can hear you saying, 'all this may be true, but I should need months or years of study to verify it all, and meanwhile life is short! Isn't there a quicker way for me to recognize the Catholic Church as the one founded by Christ?'

Think of the *visible continuity* of the Catholic Church. Jesus Christ said that He was founding a Church against which the power of Hell couldn't prevail; a Church that couldn't be destroyed. He also said that His Church would be visible throughout the world, just as a city on a hill-top is visible for miles around. In fact He compared His Church to many visible things, like a sheepfold or a huge tree. The very word, 'Kingdom,' denotes something public and visible, with office-holders and those whom they govern.

Now, Jesus Christ, as I think you're willing to believe, is God incarnate. Therefore He was able to found a Church that would be what He said it was going to be: visible and perpetual. Only the Catholic Church fulfils these requirements. I mentioned last time that the groups called 'Protestant', which claim to be based on 'the Bible alone', are relatively recent developments. They all descend from the men in the sixteenth century who called themselves 'reformers', men like Martin Luther and John Calvin; or else from more recent founders still. But if they came into being then, they clearly hadn't been in existence since the time of Christ; therefore, they cannot be His Church.

Of course, these founders or reformers would say that the Church had fallen into corruption by their time, and that they were restoring her to her pristine state. But what do they mean by 'corruption'? If they mean that the primitive Church had been corrupted in the way that a living body is corrupted when it dies and is eaten by worms, then they're claiming that the Church of Christ had at some point ceased to exist. But this is against the promise of Christ to remain with His Church always. But if they simply mean that the Church, whilst remaining the Church, had lost some of her beauty or vigour, we'd have to ask those men, 'then why did you leave the Church?' For it's certain that at the Reformation in the sixteenth century, men like Luther and Calvin left the Catholic Church, a visible society governed by bishops in union with the pope, and founded new societies with different governors. Yet if they believed that they'd been brought up in the true Church of Christ, and if this Church seemed to them lacking in holiness, the right course for them was to have stayed in the Church and worked to amend what was amiss. They weren't Jesus Christ, that they should be able to found a Church to rival His; nor did they work any miracles, to show that God now wanted men to leave the Church that He had formerly founded and join another.

These men might answer me by saying, 'We didn't found a new Church; we simply set free the Church that was being oppressed by the tyranny of the pope and his supporters.' In other words, they might deny that the visible society governed by the pope was the true Church of Christ. But then we should have to ask them, 'In your opinion, where was the true Church of Christ before your Reformation? It must have existed somewhere, since Christ said that He would always stay with His Church. You reject some of our doctrines, such as confession and praying to the saints; but they're the doctrines that have been publicly taught by the pope and bishops, as you yourselves admit, for many hundreds of years. Which Church taught your doctrines in past generations? Where for example was there a Church that denied, as you deny, that the bishops are the successors of the apostles whom all Christians must follow? If there was one, history doesn't know of it.'

And if these men protested, 'Yet there were always, we believe, some men, here and there, who held our doctrines in their heart, though they couldn't profess them openly, for fear of the pope', we should have to say, 'Then what has become of the visible church founded by Jesus Christ? Your hypothetical, scattered *true believers* don't look much like a city set on a hill!'

In other words, my friend, the very fact that a religious

society came into existence some time *after* Christ shows that it can't be the visible Church He came to found. But you don't need a long study of history to see that whilst the non-Catholic bodies were founded by some person or group after the time of the apostles, the Catholic Church can trace her history right back to the foot of Christ's cross.

Finally, you might be wondering, if things really are so simple, how anyone could have dared to leave the Catholic Church and found a new one. Yet remember how easily men are led by their passions rather than their reason. Intellectual vanity, ambition, desire for power, anger and lust are all great forces – especially if they can be harnessed by the fallen spirits (there can be provocation, too, from bad Catholics.) And once the break with the Church has been made, and new societies formed, they tend to become permanent, as it's natural for men to remain in the religious group in which they were born. But the Holy Spirit is always at work to draw those who seek the truth back towards the undivided Church of Christ.

With best wishes,
Christophorus

Letter Twenty-One

ON THE POPE

Dear Ali,

You say you're fairly convinced that the Protestant groups don't correspond to the permanent, visible Church that Christ said He would found. But you want to know what to think of the 'Orthodox Christians', such as we find especially in Greece and Russia. You write, 'They seem to be able to trace their Church back to the time of the apostles, and they have many millions of members. Don't they have just as good a claim as the Catholic Church to be the Church that Christ founded? Or should one perhaps say that Christ's Church has fallen into two halves, one called "Catholic", the other "Orthodox"?'

To answer your last question first, I don't believe one can say that Christ's Church has fallen into two halves. Apart from the fact that the Catholic 'half' would be much bigger than the other one, Christ said that His Church wouldn't be destroyed. But if it had been broken into a Catholic and an Orthodox part, it would no longer truly exist. Remember that the Church is a *visible* society. It's a 'Kingdom', as Jesus Christ so often said. But the Catholics and the Orthodox don't form one visible society. According to the philosophers, every society exercises three powers. It has a legislative power, to establish laws; an executive power, to deploy its resources; and a judicial power to maintain its good order. On each of these tests, we must say that Catholics and Orthodox form two societies, not one. So if neither of them is the true Church of Christ, we'd have to say that this Church no longer exists anywhere in the world.

In fact, what is called 'the Orthodox Church' is not really one society itself. It's more like a federation of independent national bodies. There's no overall head of the Orthodox Church with power to take decisions or enact laws binding on all who belong to it. What's more, at any given time, one national church within the federation may be in serious disagreement with another, even to the point that their priests or bishops refuse to worship together.

This brings us to another important mark of the Church founded by Christ, *unity*. Even if we'd never heard of the pope, we might guess that if God wished to found a visible society that would endure to the end of time, outlasting all human empires and surviving every crisis of civilization, He would give it some very strong principle of *unity*. For a thing only *is*, insofar as it is *one*. I think we might guess that a Church spread out across all the nations would need some strong central authority in order to keep it together.

Things might be different for a religion, like Judaism, which one enters simply by being born of a certain physical stock; for there the fact of common descent ensures that the religion will keep some kind of unity, if only an imperfect one. Or again, if a religion consists only of a very small number of doctrines, and these are naturally familiar to mankind, such as the existence of one God, then it may retain its unity without the help of a visible head. But a religion such as Christianity that contains many doctrines which surpass human understanding, membership in which depends not on physical descent but on common acceptance of all its doctrines, must, if it is to spread through time and space, have some strong and visible principle of unity in order to hold together for more than a very few years. Otherwise, disagreements about the mysterious doctrines that it teaches would soon fracture it into many parts. But then how could the Church be a city set on a hill and a light to the nations?

In other words, even if Christ had said nothing about giving His followers a visible head to ensure their unity, we'd have been justified in supposing that He, as Wisdom incarnate, would have done so. But in fact, one of the most striking things in all four of the Gospels, as I expect you've already noticed, is the place that Christ accords to St Peter. It's clear that he was the chief apostle. For example, when the angel speaks to the women at Christ's tomb after the Resurrection, he instructs them to tell 'the disciples and Peter' that Christ is risen. That's in St Mark's Gospel. In St Luke's Gospel, at the Last Supper, Christ tells the twelve apostles that Satan desires to gain power over them, but that He has prayed for Peter so that Peter's faith might not fail; and He commands Peter to strengthen the rest of the apostles. St John records that when Christ met St Peter, who at that time was called Simon, He said that he would later receive a new name, 'Petros' or 'Cephas', which are the Greek and Aramaic words respectively for 'rock'.

St Matthew records how this name was actually bestowed (I quoted the start of this passage in an earlier letter.) When Jesus Christ asks His followers who they think He is, all the other apostles remain silent, but Peter suddenly speaks up and says, 'You are the Christ, the Son of the living God.' Christ tells him that he's answered correctly, not from his own native wit, but as directly inspired by Heaven. He then says:

> I say to you that you are Peter, and on this rock I will build my Church. ... I will give you the keys of the kingdom of heaven. Whatever you bind on earth shall be bound in heaven, and whatever you loose on earth shall be loosed in heaven.

Christ declares that this apostle, whom He now names Peter or 'rock', will be the rock on which His whole Church is built. He'll keep the Church together after Christ's ascension into heaven, somewhat as the foundations of a house prevent the house from collapsing. St Peter's decisions about the running of the Church were to be final, since he held the 'keys' that bind and loose, that is, the authority to decide on disputed questions within Christ's Church.

I could go on recording texts that show the unique place of St Peter among the other apostles, but maybe I've already convinced you of it. You'll certainly find others as you read through the Gospels and the 'Acts of the Apostles'. Notice for example how Christ tells St Peter after the Resurrection to 'feed His flock', that's to say, all believers; or how Peter tells the other apostles that they must select a replacement for Judas Iscariot, who'd committed suicide.

St Peter, of course, was a mortal man, and so he

couldn't remain on earth forever as the leader of Christ's flock. He lived for about 30 years after Christ's death and Resurrection, and then he died a martyr's death, crucified in Rome by the Emperor Nero. So if Christ planned His Church wisely, He must have provided for St Peter to have a successor. After all, a house needs a foundation for as long as it's in existence, not just when it's first built. The Church on earth, composed of mortal men still sometimes subject to ambition, jealousy and other passions, needs a visible head to keep it all together.

After St Peter died, his place as chief bishop was taken by Linus, the new Bishop of Rome, and his by Cletus. That was the beginning of the series of popes which has continued in unbroken succession down to the present day. The pope is the head of the Church on earth. He's the successor of St Peter. The popes are only mortal men, but they have an authority that comes to them directly from Jesus Christ.

The pope must watch over Christ's flock, just as St Peter was told to do. He sees that bishops are appointed in all parts of the world. He takes care that no false ideas about faith or morals spread among Catholics. Sometimes he writes letters to all the bishops, or to all the faithful, or even to those outside the Church who are willing to listen, telling them about what God has revealed through Christ.

In other words, the Catholic Church, alone among the world-wide religious societies that bear the name of 'Christian', has a visible head such as men require if they are to remain united. Only in the Catholic Church do we find retained that structure which Christ gave to his apostles, with the pope raised above the other bishops as St Peter was raised above the other apostles, having responsibility for the whole flock. Neither the Orthodox Churches, nor the Anglican Communion, nor the Methodists, nor the Lutherans, nor the Baptists, nor the 'Evangelicals', even claim, as we do, to be governed by the successor of St Peter.

So I hope you can see how the Catholic Church is simply the continuation throughout time of that body of disciples and other believers whom Jesus Christ gathered around Him, which He left in St Peter's charge after the Resurrection. The other Christian groups, however admirable some of their members may be, are separated, some more, some less, from this visible Church founded by the Son of God.

With best wishes,

Christophorus

Letter Twenty-Two

ON THE UNCHANGEABLENESS OF THE FAITH

Dear Ali,

You say it's obvious to you that St Peter had a special position among Christ's disciples, and that it's reasonable to suppose that Jesus Christ would have wanted someone to take over St Peter's role as 'shepherd of the flock' after he died. But you wonder if there's not a danger, all the same, in attributing such power to a mortal man, who, as you point out, is a fallen human being. You write, 'We can't go wrong if we take Jesus Christ for a guide, if He is the Word of God incarnate. But if we take a pope for a guide, might he not lead us into sin? Catholics seem to believe whatever the pope says, since they call him 'infallible'; but what if one pope contradicts another? Do you have to change your opinions to follow his?'

To avoid any possible misunderstanding, we don't say that we have to copy the pope's behaviour. The vast majority of our 264 popes since St Peter have been, thank God, fine and virtuous men. Some are officially honoured by the Church as saints, and many of the early ones were martyred for refusing to worship false gods. Still, if a pope should ever commit a sin, we don't say that Catholics may copy him. A sin is always a sin, whoever commits it. And if a pope should ever command a person to commit a sin, which God forbid, that person would have the duty to say 'No'. God is higher than the pope, and God's law may never be contravened.

What Catholics are obliged to do, is to follow the pope's teaching. When he invokes the authority that he holds from Christ, and addressing himself to all the faithful, says 'such-and-such a thing is part of the truth revealed by Christ to the apostles' or 'this or that act is contrary to the law of God', then we must accept what he says. We hold that Christ won't let the head of His Church on earth teach anything false, when he does this.

This is what we mean by the infallibility of the pope. It doesn't mean that all his private opinions or chance remarks are necessarily true. It means that when he speaks as teacher of the universal Church, and says to all his fellow Catholics, 'This is what we must believe if we want to remain in the truth', God will not let him go wrong. Since the pope is the visible head of the Church on earth, he has the authority to say what the Church's faith is and what it isn't. If he erred when he tried to do this, he would be binding the whole Church to accept a falsehood. But then Christ's promises would have come to nothing, and the devil, 'the father of lies', would have prevailed over His flock.

So you see that the problem of one pope contradicting another doesn't arise, for Catholics. Of course, not all popes have the same private opinions as each other, even about some theological problems. Or again, a later pope will sometimes adopt a policy different from that of a predecessor in his running of the Church, for example about whether to hold diplomatic relations with some anti-Christian regime. But we hold, both as a matter of faith and as a historical fact, that no pope ever contradicts an earlier one when he teaches the whole Church about the truth revealed by God.

If you think about it, you'll see that the Church needs the pope to have this kind of infallibility, if she's to remain what St Paul calls her, 'the pillar and ground of the truth'. Given that Christ has made the pope the shepherd of His flock, whoever separates himself from the pope separates himself from Christ's flock. But if the pope taught error and told all Catholics to believe his teaching, then he'd be making error the condition of belonging to Christ's flock. One would have to choose between believing a heresy and being separated from the Church. That's impossible, if the Church is the society founded by the Son of God to show us the way to eternal life.

No group separated from the pope claims infallibility for itself in the way that the Catholic Church does. They realize that they lack a proper *organ* of infallibility, which is what the papacy is. The Orthodox Churches, for example, don't claim to teach infallibly about the new moral problems that can arise from time to time. Since they lack an organ of infallibility, they're obliged to leave such questions to their faithful to decide.

But notice that the pope can't introduce any *new* articles of faith, even though in moral questions he sometimes applies old principles to new situations. All the dogmas we need to know were taught by Jesus Christ to his twelve apostles, and these are what are passed on by the pope and the bishops in every age. But when unstable or malicious or simply confused people put some aspect of this teaching in doubt, and sow the seeds of uncertainty by the questions they ask or the statements they make, then the pope can speak up like Simon Peter, even if everyone else in authority remains silent, and recall the Christian people to the true understanding of the faith.

So Catholics don't believe that God makes new revelations through the pope, as He once did through the prophets and apostles. The pope's task is just to guard the revelation that's already been made, and to see that nothing is taken away from it, and nothing strange added to it. He doesn't do this on his own, of course. He does it in union with his brother bishops; and with all those throughout the world who help pass on the faith, whether parish priests, theology professors, catechists or the mothers and fathers of Christian children. But in controverted matters, the final judgment rests with him, and all Catholics must accept it. And yet all he's doing when he makes his final judgment is re-affirming a truth that was revealed long ago. Imagine a man who guards some precious treasure for a king while the king is in a foreign land. Just so, the pope guards 'the deposit of faith' that Christ left on earth, until He comes again.

The Church can change some of her own internal rules, for example about the languages in which a priest is allowed to conduct religious ceremonies. But, the *faith* of the Church, and her teaching on moral matters, must remain the same from age to age. If they didn't, they couldn't be from God. So this is another mark of the true Church: its teaching doesn't change to suit the opinions or prejudices of a given period, but always remains constant. One of our proudest claims as Catholics is that we hold exactly the same faith as all our forebears. We have the same faith as St Peter the fisherman of the first century, or as St Bede, the learned English monk of the eighth century, or as St Joan of Arc, the mystical peasant-girl of the fifteenth century, or as St Edith Stein, the philosopher turned nun, killed at Auschwitz in the twentieth century.

Our faith, you see, is a beginning of the life that we hope for in heaven. What the Church sees in heaven is what she believes here below. There the saints see the Blessed Trinity, and the God-Man, and the power of Christ's sacrifice, and all the other truths revealed by God. And just as the vision of the Church in heaven is unchanging, so also is the faith of the Church on earth. In fact it's part of our faith that the same faith which has come down from the apostles will be passed on whole and entire, until the last day of the world when Christ comes again. Then there will be no further need for faith, since, as the apostle St Paul says, 'God will be all in all'.

With best wishes,
Christophorus

Letter Twenty-Three

ON AN OBJECTION
TO THE LAST LETTER

Dear Ali,

You agree with me that a religion which changes its teachings can't be from God, but you wonder if the Catholic Church hasn't in fact had to revise some of her positions, even on matters of faith and morals. You write: 'In the past, you Catholics used force to promote your faith. Everyone from the pope down said it was God's will for you to put heretics to death and fight against non-Christian countries. But now everyone from the pope down says that this was all a mistake and everyone should be free to make up his own mind on matters of faith. This seems like quite a big turnaround.'

I don't think that's really a true picture; but let's take things slowly. We hold and always have held that *no one must be forced to become a Christian*. Baptism must always be a free choice. If someone agreed to baptism not because he had faith in Christ but because he was afraid of being killed, then his baptism wouldn't help him or the Church, nor would it give any glory to God. What's more, the man who forced him to become a Christian would commit a serious offence against God. That's why, in the days of Christendom, the Church insisted that

Catholic princes were not to use force on unbaptized people within their realms – normally Jews – to make them into Christians.

But this doesn't mean that the State should be uninterested in religion. It's true we say that there should be a distinction between Church and State, in the sense that the same people shouldn't normally govern both; but that's not to say that the State should be 'neutral' in religious matters. Distinction, after all, doesn't mean total separation. In fact, many popes, including twentieth century ones, have taught that the State should promote true religion.

The State, you see, is part of God's plan. He wants us to live in society. But since God's plan is unified, and since its final goal is for us to live with Him in glory, He must want human societies to help us reach this goal. In fact, a State can't ever be truly neutral. A country's laws and customs will either make the road to salvation harder or easier. What Jesus Christ said of individuals can also be applied to societies: 'the one who is not for me is against me'. This is why the popes have taught that wherever possible, the State should support the true religion officially. And since we believe that Catholicism is the true religion, shouldn't the State, where possible, officially establish the Catholic Church? But if this can't be done, then the State should still make sure that Catholics may freely practise their religion.

This last point explains what the crusader wars were about, at least on the Catholic side. They weren't an attempt to convert people by force, but to gain freedom for Catholics to pursue the religion which, we believe, comes from God Himself. Those Christian knights, for example, who fought in Palestine in the Middle Ages, weren't sent by the pope to convert anyone by force, but to 'liberate the holy places'. That's to say, Christians were being prevented from going on pilgrimage to the sites of our Lord's life. The Crusaders fought so that Christians might be free to worship God the Blessed Trinity in the places where Jesus Christ Himself once walked.

But now, consider a State where the vast majority of citizens is Catholic and where the Church has been established by law as the official religion of the country. In such a society, the Catholic faith itself would be a bond between the citizens. It might be – it ought to be – the greatest such bond, but in any case it would be an important one. Any people in such a society who weren't Christians and weren't trying to undermine the Church would be left in peace. But in a truly Catholic society, those who positively attacked Catholicism couldn't just be ignored, since they'd be threatening the cohesion of society itself (they'd be like people today who preach racial hatred). This would be true whether they were attacking Catholics with physical violence, or through books, television programmes, visits from house to house, or some other means. The civil authorities could legitimately prevent such people from assaulting Catholicism in this way. They could do this for two good reasons: to maintain the body politic in unity and peace, and to ensure that their society helped people, as God wishes, to reach eternal life.

This applies to any Catholic society, whether in the Middle Ages or today. Of course there's room for disagreement about what measures should actually be taken against those who try to undermine the faith of

Catholics. In the Middle Ages the death penalty was used for repeated offenders, on the ground that heresy was a form of treason. How would a Catholic state that took its responsibilities seriously deal with this question today? It's difficult to say, so unused have most Catholics become to defending their religion with the help of law. But if a Catholic society of the kind I've sketched above were restored in England, for example, I'd make two predictions: those trying repeatedly to undermine Catholicism would be dealt with according to the ideas then current about what constitutes a just punishment for a serious offence; and churchmen would tend to support the claims of mercy above those of justice.

In recent years, the popes and the other bishops have had to deal with a new question, unknown in the past: how should they respond to atheistic States which repress all religion? Since the rulers of these countries accept no deity or revelation, the popes haven't generally told them that they must allow Catholicism because it's revealed by God. Rather, they've insisted on man's natural right to practise religion. This right follows from our possession of an intellect and a will, which enable us to think about where we come from and what our duties are. Since this is a natural right, it belongs to all human beings whatever, even before they've embraced Christianity. For example, people on a remote island who've never heard of Christ have the right to worship God, in private and in public, and the civil authorities on that island, if there are any, mustn't try to stop them. On the other hand, I don't see how this right can be invoked in favour of *false* beliefs, since a 'right' sounds like it must be a claim to something *good*. In any case, though the Church says there's a natural right to practise religion, she doesn't teach now, any more than in the Middle Ages, that a right exists to spread ideas subversive of the Catholic faith. After all, as St Paul says, 'Christ must reign': in our hearts especially, but also in our schools and streets and parliaments and courts.

So, in the ideal Catholic society, no one would be forced to become a Catholic, and non-Christians would be free to follow their religion at home and with their families, as was done in the Middle Ages. But people wouldn't be allowed to try to draw Catholics away from Christ's Church, since that would be to draw them away from salvation. Wouldn't a State do something if it knew that men were poisoning its reservoirs? False ideas about God and man are a kind of poison too, deadly not for the body but for the spirit.

With best wishes,
Christophorus

Letter Twenty-Four

ON THE SACRAMENTS

Dear Ali,

You say that you want to hear more now about what it's actually like to *be* a Catholic. 'It seems to me', you write, 'that Catholics have a lot of intermediaries between themselves and God, such as the Church, priests, the pope and so on, whereas other Christians just relate to God directly by praying and reading the Bible. Is that so?'

I don't think that's exactly so, since our faith certainly teaches us that we must pray to God directly. Our personal relationship to Him is all-important; it determines our lot for eternity. Simply belonging to the Church and even going to Mass every Sunday won't save us if we're unwilling to love God above all else. On the other hand, in practice if not in theory, the average Protestant does make use of intermediaries in his practice of religion. He generally relies on his pastor, for example, to explain the Scriptures to him, even if according to his own principles he's free to accept what the pastor says or reject it. In the same way, when he's in some time of great need, he'll probably ask people to pray for him – and what are we doing when we pray for someone, if not becoming intermediaries between that person and God?

Still, I think your remark about the difference between

Catholics and others has got hold of something true. As well as having a personal relationship with God our Father, we also set a lot of store by intermediaries of various kinds. Why is this?

Remember that Christianity starts with our need for an intermediary. Our religion is based on the fact that *we can't save ourselves*. If you remember this, I think you'll be a good way towards having an answer to your question, 'what is it like to be a Catholic?' Simply put, since the Fall of Man, we are in a hole, and by ourselves, we can't come out.

We can't save ourselves: but God wants to save us. That's why He became man for us. Perhaps you know that we call Jesus Christ our 'mediator'? This means that He 'stands in the middle' between men and God. Of course He's not half-way between *being* man and God. He's true God and true man. But even as a man He's set above the rest of our race. So He's in a unique position to mediate between the rest of mankind and God. That's what He did on earth, especially from the Cross, and this is also what He does in Heaven. He's our great 'Intermediary'.

So our Christian faith teaches us that we can't reach eternal life by our own efforts. We're dependent on Christ, our Mediator. We're dependent both on what He did for us while He was on earth, and on what He does for us now in heaven.

But even though Jesus Christ died for us all and now intercedes for us in heaven, we're not saved automatically. Do you remember that when I was talking about Christ's death on the Cross, I said that in reward for His obedience He 'merited' grace for all mankind? That's true, but this grace still has to be given to individual men and women. Otherwise, the whole human race would go to heaven infallibly on the grounds that Christ died for us all. And this isn't so. In other words, we need some *means* by which Christ's merits will benefit us individually, and restore grace to our souls.

What is this means? Could it just be something that we ourselves do? For example, somebody once told you that our salvation is guaranteed 'provided we believe that Christ is the Son of God and that He died for us on the Cross'. Is that all that's needed?

Certainly, God could have arranged things in this way. He could have ordained that everyone would be saved simply by his own act of believing, without need for anything more. But that might have been dangerous. Christians could easily have become proud, if they knew that they could take hold of Christ's merits simply by their own decision.

In any case, the Church tells us that God has appointed a special means by which Christ's graces will flow into our souls. God doesn't want us just to do or believe something in order to be saved; He also wants us to *receive* something. After all, God knows full well how easily human beings become proud. So He's always on the look out, so to speak, for ways to keep us humble. And so He provides certain 'channels', not of our own choosing, where we must go to receive His grace. Just as new-born children must go to their mother's breast to find their nourishment, so Christians must go to their Mother the Church to find the channels of heavenly grace that God has created within her.

These are the seven sacraments of the Church. I've

already mentioned the first of them, Holy Baptism. It's the first of the sacraments, because in baptism God restores in our soul the divine life that we lost in Adam. But one thing that baptism has in common with the other sacraments is that we must *receive* it. No one can baptise himself.

After all, Jesus Christ told us that unless we turn and become as little children we can't enter His Father's kingdom. So just as children receive what they need from their parents, we acquire God's graces not just by our own will-power, but by receiving them from Christ and the Church.

That's why the sacraments all involve things that we can see and hear. God could have washed us clean from original sin by a wholly spiritual process, but instead He uses baptismal water and the words spoken by the priest. This isn't because He's lacking in power and needs the help of His creatures! But He knows that it's natural for us to understand spiritual things by means of bodily things, and He likes to treat us gently, in accordance with our nature. So He gives us grace, something we can't see, by means of baptismal water, which we can see. So it is with all the sacraments of the Church.

Really, in the sacraments, God is completing the process that He began with the Incarnation. Two thousand years ago He sent us a Man, as a visible bridge between us and Himself. Now that Christ is in glory, and no longer visible to our mortal eyes, God gives us the seven sacraments, as so many visible bridges to Jesus Christ.

And baptism is the first of these. It's called the 'gateway' to the sacraments, since no one has the power to receive any of the other sacraments unless he's first baptised. It's so important that Jesus Himself chose to be baptized when He began His public life. Of course He didn't need it for Himself, as He was sinless. He did it to leave an example for mankind. It's as if He was saying, 'If I, though the Son of God, began my work as the Christ by receiving a form of baptism, how much more must men begin their lives as Christians by receiving baptism for themselves!'

So, to go back to your original comment, the sacraments, and the priests who administer them, are indeed intermediaries between ourselves and God. But they don't get in the way of our personal relation with Him. They make it possible, by bringing us His grace. After all, if we have a friend waiting for us on the other side of a deep river, we shouldn't complain that the bridge gets in the way between us and him! It helps us to arrive where he is. And we have many rivers to cross before we reach our homeland.

With best wishes,
Christophorus

Letter Twenty-Five

ON HOLY BAPTISM

Dear Ali,

You say that you understand the principle of the sacraments as channels by which grace comes from Jesus to us, but that you still have some doubts about them. 'Can something so simple as pouring water over a person's head really have the effect that Christians claim? It seems like a very easy way to get rid of original sin.' And a bit further on you ask, 'Isn't there a danger that Catholics will rely too much on the sacraments of the Church, and not bother about trying to lead good lives? For example, they know that whatever sins they commit, they can go to confession afterwards.'

Your first question reminds me of an episode in the Old Testament. There was a Syrian called Naaman who was the head of the Syrian army, but also a leper. He heard that there was a prophet in Israel, called Elisha, who'd worked many miracles, and so even though the Syrians didn't much care for the Jews, he made the long journey to Elisha to ask him if he could heal him of leprosy. But when Naaman arrived there, the prophet didn't come out of his house to greet him. He simply sent a messenger to tell Naaman to wash seven times in the River Jordan nearby. Naaman, who was a great personage, was offended at being dealt with in such a casual way, and he said in an angry tone to his servants: 'I thought he would surely have come out to me and invoked the name of the Lord his God, and waved his hand over the place! Are not the rivers of Damascus better than all the waters of Israel?' – as if to say, if it was just a matter of washing, I could have done that at home.

But his servants were wiser than their master, and they spoke to him thus: 'Father, if the prophet had asked you to do some great thing, surely you would have done it. How much rather what he has now said to you, "Wash, and be clean".' Naaman felt the force of their words, so he swallowed his pride and went to the river. Then, the Bible says, 'he went down and washed in the Jordan seven times, and his flesh was restored, like the flesh of a little child.'

Do you see how this applies to your question? Naaman wanted the great prophet Elisha to show himself visibly and perform a dramatic ritual over him. So too we might have expected that Christ would show himself in a visible fashion when He infuses grace into our souls, or that He might at least send some sign, such as fire from heaven, upon the one being made a child of God. But instead, like Elisha, He remains hidden and sends an ordinary messenger, his priest, to the one desiring to be healed. And just as Naaman was cured by bathing not in one of the mighty rivers of the East but in the humble River Jordan, so a little water is all that's needed for the miracle of baptism to occur.

The story of Naaman, you see, is all about humility. This powerful general, so used to commanding others, has to obey someone else if he's going to be cured. And he has to obey even though he's not asked to do some heroic action that might have appealed to his warrior's heart. God, speaking through Elisha, asks him precisely to do something so trivial that it seems to Naaman humiliating. *That*, for Naaman, is the real test of obedience: will he obey purely and simply because God commands it, even though the action may demean him in the eyes of the world? After all, it must have been a rather strange sight, for a man to go in and out of the same river seven times!

So one of the reasons why God made the first sacrament so easy is that it should be a test of humility for those who approach it (another reason is so that anyone may receive it quickly if he is dying). If God had asked us to fast for many days or to make a journey on foot to Jerusalem in order to receive His holy grace, surely we should have done so. How much more if He only asks us to have a stream of water poured on our heads, while the name of the Trinity is invoked.

As for your other question, whether Catholics may rely too much on the sacraments, and forget to try to be good people, well, I suppose it may happen in some cases. But if it did, that would show that those Catholics didn't really grasp what the sacraments are. They're channels of grace, set up by Christ Himself, true; but we can block up our end of the channel. If we approach the sacraments with unbelieving hearts, or with sins that we're not willing to give up, they won't bring many graces into our souls.

The sacraments give us strength to live as children of God, but they're not a way to 'by-pass' the moral life. Nor do they take away all our capacity for sinning. When someone's baptized, the Holy Spirit comes into his soul and makes him a child of God. But he can't claim that his final salvation is infallibly assured. It says in our Scriptures, 'the Holy Spirit of discipline will flee from the deceitful, and shall not abide when iniquity comes in.' And our Lord said to His apostles, 'If anyone abide not in me, he shall be cast forth as a branch and shall wither.' If the baptized man commits some serious sin by deliberately breaking God's Law, then the Spirit of Christ won't remain inside his soul.

It's true that God has given us a means of receiving the Holy Spirit once more. As you've heard, one of the seven sacraments of the Church is the sacrament of penance, where Catholics can confess their sins and be forgiven. But this isn't 'an easy way out'. For one thing, many people find it difficult to confess their sins to a priest (humility again, you see). And then, even when we've received this sacrament of penance, we still have to perform works of reparation. No one has to do works of reparation for sins committed before baptism, since baptism washes everything away. But if we sin afterwards, then even when we're forgiven, we have to fast and pray and give alms, to make up to God for our sins.

The sacraments are wonderful helps towards heaven. In fact, Christ made them a necessary part of our journey there. He told Nicodemus, 'unless you are born again of water and the Holy Spirit, you will not enter the kingdom of Heaven.' But they shouldn't make Catholics complacent about finally arriving. Our Lord also said, 'Of those to whom much has been given, much will be expected.' God has certainly given us very much: the merits of Christ and the means to receive them into our souls. That gives us the responsibility of becoming saints.

With best wishes,
Christophorus

Letter Twenty-Six

ON FASTING AND FORBIDDEN FOODS

Dear Ali,

Your last letter made me smile a bit, when you wrote, 'I'm surprised to learn that Catholics have to fast to make up for the sins they commit after their baptism. I didn't realize that Christians ever practised fasting.' You ask what rules Christ gave us on this subject. You also want to know how to answer those who say that fasting is pointless, and that all God requires of us is to avoid gluttony. How does it please God, you wonder, that I should feel hungry? Finally, you want to know if there are any kinds of food forbidden to Christians.

I'll answer your last question first. No, there are no foods that we're forbidden to eat. Before Christ came, God willed that there should be a chosen people, the Jews, into which His Son would be born. This people had to be kept distinct from the other peoples of the earth, and so God gave it many distinguishing features. One of these was that the Jews were forbidden certain foods. However, after Jesus's Resurrection, God willed that all men should be invited to join His new chosen people, the Church. Since the Church is meant for everyone, its members don't need to distinguish themselves from other people by only eating certain foods. What's more, no food can possibly be unclean or impure in itself, since all of them were created by the good God.

Did Christ give the apostles any precise rules about fasting? To be honest, I don't know. There are none recorded in the Gospels, though that's not to say that He didn't leave some for them to follow after the Resurrection. What He did leave us, in the first place, was His example. Before He embarked upon His public ministry, He spent forty days fasting in the wilderness. St Luke tells us that He ate nothing during those days.

Christ's disciples didn't fast whilst He was on earth. When some of the stricter Jews challenged them about this, He stepped in and defended them, saying, 'Can the children of the bridegroom [that's to say, the bridegroom's friends and helpers] fast whilst the bridegroom is with them?' It was as if He was saying, 'My time on earth is not a time for men to fast but rather to be glad, for I have come like a bridegroom to be wedded to my Church.' Yet He added these words, 'But the days will come, when the bridegroom shall be taken away from them; then they shall fast in those days.' That was a reference to His ascension into heaven, when His visible presence was taken from the disciples. After the Ascension, the disciples did fast, as you'll find in the Acts of the Apostles.

Catholics consider that the Church has the right to lay down certain days or seasons when we must fast if we can. Also, since God hasn't revealed any *definite* days on which fasting must take place, we believe that the Church has the power to adapt her rules from one age to another.

One practice that's come down to us, I suppose from

the apostles, is to keep the time before Easter as a fast. This season, as you know, is called 'Lent', and it lasts for forty days, in memory of Jesus Christ's forty days' fast in the desert. At the present time, the Church only lays down as an *obligation* that two of these forty should be fast days. But she also says that Catholics should undertake voluntary penances throughout this time, and one of the best, as well as the most traditional, is to try to fast every day. Of course, 'fasting' here doesn't mean taking no food at all – we don't expect God to sustain us by a miracle! It means taking considerably less food: only one full meal in a period of twenty four hours. Only we never fast on Sundays, since every Sunday is a celebration of Christ's rising from the dead.

As well as Lent, the Church says that on every Friday of the year, unless a great feast falls that day, Catholics must not necessarily fast, but at least do some penance, such as eating no meat. This is in honour of Christ's crucifixion. And there are other days too where there is no obligation, today, to do penance, but which are traditionally days of fasting and abstaining from meat. For example, there are the 'Four Times', the 'Ember days' that occur near the beginning of each of the four seasons of the year.

Now, the Church doesn't regard fasting as the main mark of a Christian. The main mark of a Christian should be *love*. Certain people, such as the sick or the elderly, can't fast, but love isn't beyond anyone's reach. Again, it's possible that someone might fast with a proud heart, or whilst nourishing anger against another person, and that person's fast doesn't glorify God. Love, on the other hand, by which I mean love of God and of our neighbour for His sake, always glorifies the Most High. It's by love that we most resemble Him, who loves all that He has made.

So in regard to your other question, about why fasting is a good action, we need to understand that it's not an end in itself. As one of our most plain-speaking saints, St Jerome, once remarked, 'God is not delighted by the rumbling of my belly'! Fasting is only useful when it's a means to the real end of our life, love. But it does serve this end powerfully in several ways.

For one thing, fasting, like other forms of abstinence, can free the spirit a little from the body. Of course, we don't hate the body. It was made by God, and He will raise it up on the last day. But ever since the Fall, we're all too easily absorbed by what we experience through the body. Fasting helps us on the contrary to raise our spirit on high, in loving prayer to God.

Next, as you know, fasting is a way of doing penance for our sins. As I mentioned before, whenever we sin, we 'steal' from God. We deprive Him of the honour due to Him. So when we renounce something that we might lawfully have taken, such as some food, we give that thing to God, so to speak, to make up for our theft. Only don't think of this as a straightforward transaction, as if we could pay off our debts to God by our own strength. Our penances by themselves could never make up for past sins, not even if we were to fast on bread and water for forty years. But the Holy Spirit, living in the hearts of God's children, infuses our acts of penance with His own great power.

Finally, we can and should do penance *for other people*, both Christians and others. Christians are fellow 'cells' in one body, namely, Christ's. Of course, Christ's physical body is in heaven, but we call the Church His 'mystical' body. Think of what happens when we wound some part of our human body: platelets circulate to the wounded place until the bleeding stops. Or again, think of the food we digest: only one organ does the digesting, but the whole body benefits. It's the same with the Church. When one part is injured, another part can help. Charity flows between the members of the Church, just as blood circulates in our body. And just as a man's stomach, say, can do penance for a sin he committed with his tongue, so one cell in Christ's mystical body, one Christian, can do penance for another one. We don't even need to know *who* we're doing it for: God will look after that.

Yet even though penance has a special power when done by one Christian on behalf of another, we're also taught that we can do penance for anyone at all. St Paul told us to pray for those who persecute us, and every prayer is a kind of penance, since it always involves an effort to lift our minds on high. Jesus Christ offered His own life to His Father in reparation for the sins of those who killed Him, both Jews and Gentiles. In the same way we're taught to fast and do penance for our own sins, for our fellow Christians, and for those still outside the Church.

With best wishes,
Christophorus

Letter Twenty-Seven

ON THOSE
OUTSIDE THE CHURCH

Dear Ali,

Your last letter raised some big questions. You ask, 'What do Catholics say will happen to those outside the Church? Some Muslims say that all non-Muslims will go to Hell. Do you say the same about non-Catholics? Many people surely never hear about baptism or about Jesus Christ. Do they have any chance of being saved?'

As I wrote once before, when I was speaking about the 'problem of evil', God's will is simple, but when it touches our disordered world it can seem complicated, like the beam of light falling onto a shattered mirror. So we have to use many words to try to explain how God deals with mankind, as if God were complex when in fact it is we who are.

To begin, then, our faith teaches us that 'God wills all men to be saved and to come to the knowledge of the truth.' That's the unchanging beam of light, so to speak, that falls upon the human race. Mankind was meant to reflect that desire of God as perfectly as a pure mirror reflects the light of the sun. But at the beginning of time the mirror was shattered, when Adam fell. So children now are born without divine grace, and if they die in that state, before they've become responsible for their actions, they won't have the power to look upon the face of God. We believe that God will take such children into His care and see that their souls suffer no harm: but we do not count them among the blessed. That's the first complexity that sin has introduced into what would otherwise have been simple.

If a child lives, but is not baptized, what then? The Church says that God offers everyone who lives beyond infancy the possibility of entering on the way of salvation, but she doesn't go into many details about how. But I'll tell you what one of our greatest theologians said, St Thomas Aquinas, who lived in the thirteenth century.

He wrote that whenever a child lives beyond infancy, the day must come when he reflects about himself and his place in the world. He has to decide what to live for. In fact, until he does this, he's not in a position to make any free choices. All the lesser choices we make about what to do and what not to do presuppose that there's something that we love above all else. Just as we can't measure changes in temperature unless we have a thermometer whose markings don't change, so we can't decide between different actions unless we have some fixed scale of values, and some idea of what we ultimately want from life.

Now St Thomas said that whenever a boy reaches this moment of decision, he has the duty to turn to God and choose to live for Him. True, the child can't yet love God as his Father. But he can know that God exists, and desire to reach out towards Him. Even though his soul is still unsanctified, and so to speak, in the dark, he has the power to do this.

But our theologians have a saying: 'God does not deny grace to those who do what lies within them.' So St Thomas wrote that if a child, on coming to the age of reason, does all he can to direct himself to God, then God will grant that child a grace to heal him of original sin. And since Jesus Christ has said, 'No man comes to the Father except by me', I think this grace must be that Christ reveals Himself in some way to that child. Then the child can believe in Him, even if perhaps he doesn't yet know Him by name.

How often this happens, I don't know: God knows. St Thomas warns that even though God always offers the necessary help, it's not easy for an unbaptized child to turn to Him, precisely because he is without grace. So I don't see how we can suppose that it happens often. Yet it is possible, because God is good, and because He lets Himself be found by those who seek Him.

Perhaps someone might object, 'What if the child has been brought up by atheists? He can hardly turn to God if he doesn't even know that God exists!' I think our theologians might reply that every child, when he comes to the age of reason, has some kind of knowledge of God. Just by experiencing creation, the child has a spontaneous knowledge of the Creator, even if his parents and teachers have kept the word 'God' from his ears. It's only later on, when he'll be old enough to listen to sophistry, or be dominated by passions or pride, that he risks losing this early knowledge of his Maker. But while his reason is still fresh, he knows that there is a power who governs all things, whom it's right to obey.

If the child doesn't begin his moral life by turning to God, he must choose something else to be his ruling principle: probably his own happiness. If he does that, he doesn't become entirely corrupt. He'll still know right from wrong, and be able to perform some good acts. But he'll only be living a *natural* life. Even if he grows up to believe that God exists and learns to recite prayers to Him, he won't be freed of original sin, nor will he yet have a friendship with God. His soul will still be dead. Yet God can give him other opportunities to convert, sending him preachers of the Gospel later on.

But what happens to the first child, as he grows up? If Christ has revealed Himself to him, and he has believed in Him, he will also believe Christ's preachers, when he hears them. Then he'll be able to ask for baptism and truly become a child of God.

But what if he dies before hearing about the need for baptism? After all, there may be no Christians in his country, or none who speak to him about divine things. The Church says this: if it should ever happen that someone dies believing in Christ and the Holy Trinity, loving God and being sorry for his sins, yet without having been baptised, then God will not exclude such a one from heaven. For God is just, and He can never blame someone for what was not his fault.

But is such a person then saved outside the Church? No, we don't say that either. Remember that the Church isn't just a visible society, like a club or a political party. It's also the *Communion of Saints*: the union of all those who live by Christ's grace. So as soon as anyone has the smallest degree of this grace in his soul, he belongs in a certain way to the Church. His soul is inside it, we might say, even if his body isn't. And after death, if not before, he will discover the name of the great family into which he has been adopted.

With best wishes,
Christophorus

Letter Twenty-Eight

ON THOSE OUTSIDE THE CHURCH

(cont'd.)

Dear Ali,

You write as follows: 'Apparently it's very hard for an unbaptized child to turn to God; but if he doesn't, he remains without God's grace. So if God really desires the salvation of all human beings, why does He allow so many children to be born outside Christian families, and in countries where they may never meet a Catholic priest? Is it fair on them?'

My friend, we cannot hope to know the reasons of all God's actions in particular. That is something we shall only see on the last day. So if you ask me why *this* child is born into *this* society and has *these* teachers, then I can't tell you. But if you are asking me, as a general question, why God allows so many to be born and raised outside the Church, then I can offer you some general answers, or at least, suggestions.

The first question is surely, why is the Church herself not more widespread? For one could hardly expect God by a miracle to prevent non-Christian parents from having children! So let's try to answer this first question first.

Do you remember what I said when we spoke of original sin? I wrote that it's only because God honoured our first father so highly that his sin affects us so deeply. God gave Adam the possibility of being the spiritual father of the whole race. He gave him the power to pass on many good things to us: but this meant that his fall deprived us of those same good things. We can say something similar about the spread of the Church. God has made Christians into His adopted children. He gives us the power of spreading His kingdom. He honours us in this way for the sake of His Son, whose name we bear. But it follows that if Christians are unfaithful to their calling, through laziness or sin, then God's kingdom suffers. If God has *really* given us the power to co-operate with Him in spreading the Church, then necessarily, if we do not co-operate, the Church will not be spread, and if we only co-operate in a lukewarm manner then the Church will only be spread slowly.

It's true that it's not easy for an unbaptized child to turn to God when he reaches the age of reason. But then it's not *easy* for a baptized child to remain in grace all his life long. Salvation is always difficult. As Job said, 'Man's life on earth is a warfare.' Salvation can never be easy, because we're made of both flesh and spirit, and these two don't tend in the same direction. No doubt, a Catholic has special remedies to help him if he falls, such as the sacrament of confession. Yet if he doesn't use what's offered to him, and especially if he rejects it with contempt, then he may fall to a worse state than many an unbaptized person. The very fact that he's received such blessings from God makes his sins more serious. So it may be easier for an unbaptized person to find pardon after a certain sin than it would be for a baptized person who has committed the same sin, and then rejected the Church's remedies. Jesus Christ said: 'Of those to whom much has been given, much is expected.' It follows that less is expected of those to whom less is given.

For example, in some places women were taught from childhood that it was a wife's duty to die on her husband's funeral pyre. If a woman honestly believed this, then she surely wouldn't have been condemned for dying in this way, even though a Christian knows that suicide is always forbidden. So Christians expect to be judged more strictly than others.

But you want to know more about how God deals with those who never hear the Gospel. Let's imagine a country that has neither priests nor, as far as we can tell, sacraments. If God desires the inhabitants of this land to be saved, why does He leave them in such a plight? First, remember that God's desire for our salvation doesn't lessen His justice. It may be that the inhabitants of the land have sinned in some especially grievous way, or at least that many have done so. God may be leaving them without missionaries or sacraments because they have made themselves so unworthy of his gifts. For a land where the majority of the inhabitants was trying hard to keep the law that God has written on our hearts wouldn't be left for long without His preachers.

Yet even if God punishes a land by depriving it of the sacraments, his mercy will still be at work. God's justice is never found without His mercy, since in Him mercy and justice are one. God may know that if He sent missionaries to this sinful land, then the people would reject them, blaspheming the gospel, and so adding a new and worse sin to their former ones. So God, wishing to prevent them from falling further into evil, doesn't allow his missionaries to travel to that land. Or it may be that He allows their sins to grow so that one day they'll come to their senses, suddenly aware of their degradation. When that happens, perhaps God will finally send them His preachers.

But remember that even a land without priests or sacraments may have retained some of the original revelation that God gave first to Adam and later to Noah. So the people may know that there is one God, that He alone is to be worshipped, that He loves justice, and that He will judge all men according to their deeds. Perhaps some of the people, guided by this primitive revelation, are 'feeling after God', as St Paul puts it. Their efforts aren't enough to save them, true: but a man who offers sincere prayers and tries to act justly to his fellows surely attracts God's mercy to himself, even if his nation might seem to be forsaken.

After all, just as every human being stands before God at the beginning of his moral life, so must it often be at the end. I don't mean at the judgment after death, for then there'll no longer be opportunity for anyone to convert. I mean in the last moments before death. Who knows what passes in a soul when a man lies unconscious, no longer able to communicate even with his friends? Surely the soul becomes more aware of God as its senses begin to be sealed up, and it prepares to depart from the body. Maybe Christ uses these moments to make good the deficiencies of His preachers, and comes in person to those who have never heard the gospel. Maybe He lets the approach of death humble those who might have refused His message whilst they were still vigorous and ambitious, but who are now ready to receive it. Are there people who have lived without faith in Him all their lives, but who come to know Him at the very end? Why not? How many, only God knows.

Of course these are only speculations. Christ told the apostles to preach the gospel to all nations, and that's what the Church tries to do. All I've been trying to show you is that there's no contradiction between God's desire to save all mankind through His Son and the actual state of the world, where families, villages and sometimes even whole countries may not hear the public preaching of the gospel, at least for a time. God's arm is not made short, and He can help anyone who truly seeks Him. Yet all the same, Catholics fear for those who haven't yet entered the Church, and we constantly pray God to save them.

With best wishes,
Christophorus

Letter Twenty-Nine

ON PRAYER

Dear Ali,

You say that you're puzzled by what I wrote at the end of my last letter, that Catholics ask God to send missionaries to people who haven't yet heard the gospel. 'Does God need persuading to do this? Surely if God sees that a certain city or country will benefit, on the whole, from having the gospel preached there, He will send it missionaries; if He sees that it won't benefit, He won't send them. If God is good, why is it necessary for people to pray? Wouldn't He just do it without being asked?'

I think that your question conceals a fallacy. It's as if you're saying, 'Since God is good and all-powerful, He must always give His creatures the best possible chances of salvation.' If that were true, then I'd agree with your objection; it would be superfluous for us to ask God to spread the knowledge of Christianity throughout the earth. In fact, if we followed the logic of your objection to the end, it would be superfluous for us to ask God to do anything at all. Since He's perfect, He'd always give the best possible things to His creatures, and there'd be no need for anyone to ask Him. Or if it were necessary to ask God for something, this would seem to show that

He's not perfect, since He would need persuading before giving His creatures what's best.

Now I say that this is all fallacious, and for a simple reason: *God can always do something better than what He does*. There's no such thing as 'the best of all possible worlds'. However good a world God makes, He could always make a better one, since He's almighty. Likewise, there's no such thing as the 'greatest number of helps to salvation', or 'the most powerful graces', since whatever helps and graces that God gives to men, He could always give greater and more powerful ones. If He couldn't, then He would no longer be God. However many times God has offered the grace of repentance to someone who's disobeyed His commands, He can always offer him this grace once more.

So when we pray to God, and ask Him to give light to those who don't yet know Him, we're not suggesting that God's generosity is in need of being supplemented by our prayers. It's just the other way around. It's because God's generosity is unlimited that we know that He can always give something more in response to our prayers. So Jesus Christ has told us that we 'ought always to pray, and not lose heart'.

'Do we hope to change God's mind by our prayers?', you wonder. No, because God is immutable. Since He's above time, He's not to be changed by prayer or by anything else. But God sees our prayers from all eternity; in fact, all that's good in our prayers is caused by Him, though if we pray selfishly or foolishly, this is from ourselves. And He chooses that our prayers should affect what happens in creation. Take some event that we might say was the answer to a prayer, for example Catholic missionaries arriving in Japan. We don't say that the Church prayed for the spread of the gospel, and that as a result God decided that missionaries should go to Japan. Rather, we say that God willed that the missionaries should arrive in Japan *on account of prayer* – and not without it.

Remember that our relation to God is a personal one. When we've been made His children through baptism, we have the right to speak to Him with all the confidence of a child speaking to a loving Father – though always with reverence as well. A good human father will give many things to his children without being asked, but sometimes he'll wait for the child to ask before he gives. And this isn't necessarily because the father doesn't know what his child needs. He may see perfectly well that his son or daughter needs help with homework, for example. But he may wait to be asked before he gives the help. Perhaps he wants the child to ask spontaneously, as a sign of its trust in him. Or perhaps the child is proud and wilful, and would reject the help if it were offered straightaway, even though he needs it. The father may want the child to learn humility by struggling for a while until finally giving in and turning to him for help.

This helps us to understand how God treats us. All that we receive could have come to us without a single prayer. But God has decided otherwise. He's chosen that some of the things that His creatures receive will come to them as a result of prayer. Sometimes it's our own prayers that bring us God's blessings; sometimes it's the prayers that other people make for us, even without our being aware of it. God wants us to have the experience of praying for something and then gaining it, so that our trust in Him may grow. If a child found that his father corrected his homework as soon as he was puzzled by some question, he might be glad of it, but it wouldn't help to create a personal relationship between the two of them. But if he turns to his father spontaneously and asks for help, and his father obliges, that will increase the child's trust.

Yet God may want us to have the experience of praying for things and *not* receiving them. Sometimes our prayers are far too casual. We can be like the child who asks for his father's help imperiously, as if he thought his father only existed to serve him. God can't answer prayers like this; it would be contrary to His own holiness, as well as bad for our salvation. Instead, He humbles us by not granting our request, until we've learned to pray with more reverence for His name.

Sometimes our prayers aren't answered immediately, not because they're blameworthy, but simply because God wants us to make spiritual progress by persevering in prayer. Every prayer made in faith causes faith to grow. Every aspiration of the soul towards God increases our desire for Him and therefore our capacity for heavenly bliss. So even if we don't receive what we ask for when we pray, our prayer will always benefit us in these other ways.

Sometimes we don't receive the thing we ask for, because God sees that it would harm us. I'm not talking about prayers for something sinful, such as prayers to be a successful thief. Obviously God can't answer 'prayers' of that kind. But let's imagine that someone prays to have a better job. There isn't anything necessarily wrong with such a prayer. Someone can legitimately desire more interesting work, or a higher salary to make his family more comfortable. Yet God may see that if he received the position he desires that he'd be at risk in some way. Perhaps the new people with whom he'd associate would all be people who laughed at Christianity, so that he might be in danger of losing his faith. Or perhaps the increase in wealth and prestige might turn his head, so that he'd forget all about the world to come and give himself up entirely to this present world.

God's 'priorities', remember, are always heaven first and earth second. If we were perfectly rational, these would be our priorities too, since what lasts for ever is obviously more important that what lasts only for a time. God desires to answer our prayers, and He takes delight in doing so, since His love for us is much deeper than that of an earthly father for his children. Evil prayers, or proud prayers, or prayers that would imperil the glory that He desires for us, He doesn't answer, or answers only in order to show us what we really need. But prayers made humbly, perseveringly, in faith, for salvation or for the things that lead to salvation, God always answers. That's why Jesus says, 'Whoever asks receives; whoever seeks finds; and to him who knocks the door is always opened.'

With best wishes,
Christophorus

Letter Thirty

ON ETERNITY

Dear Ali,

My remark that eternity is much more important than time has raised a difficulty in your mind about life after death. 'Can heaven and hell really go on *forever*? It seems to me that the saints might get bored! After all, it's part of human nature to be looking for new experiences, and what new experiences would be available to those in heaven, if heaven is the end of their journey? As for hell, I can see that some people might refuse to the very end of their lives to obey God's will, and so never be able to go to heaven. But can it really please God that they should suffer *forever* because of what they did on earth? Wouldn't it be more merciful for Him simply to annihilate them, if they refused to love Him?'

It's true that eternity is very hard for us to imagine. Yet as spiritual beings, it's natural for us to exist forever in some way or other. Just as it's a property of a bird to fly or of water to flow downhill, it's a property of a spirit to be undying. Our soul is a spirit; so perpetuity is our proper medium, just as air is for a bird or water for a whale. In this life we can only know this intellectually, by faith, or as the conclusion of an argument; but after death I believe that we shall also *feel* it. When we step into eternity, we'll realize that it's the medium for which we were made. Imagine how a fish might feel if it had been born on land and then brought for the first time to the ocean.

Be reassured, the saints in heaven won't get bored! Why do people get bored on earth? Obviously, because they don't have enough to interest them. Perhaps they only have a small circle of acquaintances, and the work they do makes no demands on their intelligence or imagination. And even those with many friends and acquaintances and with fascinating work to do can get bored sometimes, perhaps if illness prevents them from seeing people, or makes their work impossible.

But even on earth I believe that there are some people who don't get bored. Who do I mean? Those who live for God. People of that kind can never run out of things to do, since there's always something that God wills for a person to be doing. Those who live for God can certainly grow tired and feel physical and mental pain, but they won't become bored. Already on earth they're joined to the One who is the source of all joy.

If this is true for such people even on earth, how much more in heaven! There the saints won't simply be working for God; they'll *see* Him as He is. The sight of Him will more than satisfy all their desires. After all, why do people look for new experiences? Isn't it because they've only experienced limited, created things? A limited thing may satisfy us in some ways, but never in all. You've probably noticed in your own circle of friends that one friend appeals to one side of your character, another friend to another. That's why even the best of friends – even a husband and a wife – desire some time away from each other. No created thing, not even a person whom we may love more than our own life, can satisfy all our aspirations. For we were made for some infinite good.

God is that infinite good. He isn't a limited good thing, like the things we can possess on earth; He is goodness itself. So if we once 'possess' Him as the saints do in heaven, we can never desire anything else. Could that happiness ever grow stale, you wonder? No: things begin to pall on us not just because we've had them for some time, but because when their novelty wears away, it no longer hides their limitations. But with God that can never happen, for His goodness has no limitations. So Jesus Christ said, 'He that shall drink of the water that I shall give him shall not thirst for ever.'

One of our saints has said, 'God alone is enough.' You can understand that as meaning either 'nothing suffices us apart from God', or 'God suffices us even in the absence of anything else.' Even if there were only one soul in heaven, she would be blissfully happy in the company of the Blessed Trinity for all eternity. Yet in fact, as well as that happiness, the saints in heaven also have the happiness of each other's company. Even the deepest friendship on earth is only the embryo of what will be in heaven. The saints there will know each other perfectly, and each one will have a unique friendship with each of his millions of companions. No, there will be no shadow of boredom in heaven.

But what of those other souls, those who choose themselves rather than God? Remember what I said before: the moment any soul leaves its body, its 'attitude' is fixed forever. So if a soul leaves this life preferring its own will to God, this is how it will remain for eternity. You ask why a life of only 70 or 80 years, or perhaps much less, should determine the soul's fate for ever. But what is the alternative? Let's imagine that men lived for 900 years, as our sacred scriptures say that once they did. One could still raise the same objection, for what's 900 years compared to eternity? And the same would be true of 9,000 years or 90,000. However high we go, if we agree that death fixes the attitude of the soul, it follows that an eternal destiny is decided by a finite life.

Can God want any of His creatures to suffer for eternity, you ask. He can't want this for its own sake, as though suffering could please Him. But He must desire what is just, since He is justice itself. Now if a man, during his life on earth, has given himself up to ambition, whether for pleasure or power or money, what should happen to him when he dies? During his life he's been able more or less successfully to put the thought of God out of his mind. From the moment his soul leaves his body, he won't be able to do this any more. His soul resembles God, since it's a spirit, and so the existence of God will be burningly evident to it. But this soul has been fixed by death in a state of aversion from God. The soul desires that *God should not be*; that there should be no check to its own self-gratification. Yet it's now confronted by God, the supreme reality, and because it desires above all that God should not be, it is tortured by this encounter. The soul knows that it was made to be happy with God, and yet it hates Him, and it's no longer able to distract itself by any of the pleasures or pastimes that were permitted it in this life.

Now what should God do with such a soul? Should

He offer it reconciliation? The soul would refuse it. If God were to say to such a soul, 'Your sufferings will cease and you may enter heaven if you renounce your evil will and serve Me', the soul would refuse. It prefers to remain in hell forever rather than to acquiesce in serving God.

Should God annihilate it, as you suggested? He would be acting against His own wisdom if He did so. It says in the Scriptures, 'God created all things that they might be'. He made all things to reflect something of His glory. Even the lost souls and fallen spirits do that, though unwillingly. At the very least, they show forth His justice. If He annihilated them, they would no longer do so. It would be as if they had triumphed over God after all. But He would also be acting against their natures if he annihilated them. It's just as natural for a spirit to exist for ever as it is for fire to rise upwards, and God doesn't abolish the properties of the things that He's once made. He preserves the 'dignity' of His creatures, even when they rebel against Him.

There's another reason why God doesn't annihilate these evil spirits. Strange as it may sound, it's so that He may continue to have mercy on them. If they didn't exist, He could show them no more mercy; as it is, He shows some mercy even to the damned, for they don't receive as great a punishment as their hatred of Him has deserved.

We need to think about this final loss sometimes, yet not too much. Let's prefer to think of God's will that 'all should be saved, and come to the knowledge of the truth', and be with Him forever in heaven.

With best wishes,

Christophorus

Letter Thirty-One

ON MARRIAGE

Dear Ali,

After my last letter about the things of eternity you want to go back to something which is very much of this life, namely, marriage. You've heard that the Church doesn't allow Catholics to divorce, and you wonder if this isn't too severe. 'I agree,' you write, 'that divorce is always a sad thing, especially for the children. But isn't it sometimes the lesser of two evils, for example when the husband and wife are both unhappy and each would be happier with someone else?' You also want to know what we say about the relative positions of husband and wife; do they have equal rights, or is one more important? Finally, you ask why no Christian is allowed to have more than one wife, even though some of the heroes of the Old Testament, like Abraham, David and Solomon had many.

To understand what the Church says about marriage, it's good to start at the beginning, with creation. The book of Genesis says that God created the first man and first woman in His own image. Of course, men and women don't resemble the invisible God in any physical sense. We're in the image of God because we possess spiritual powers: intelligence and freedom.

This might help you to understand what we say about marriage. Since man and woman are both persons made in the image of God, neither of them can be the property of the other. The woman can't ever be the slave of the man. Scripture talks of slavery as a punishment for sin, and marriage is older than sin. After all, when God brought the first woman to the first man, He was marrying them, and that was before the Fall.

Since neither spouse is the property of the other, neither may send the other away. The wife can't be divorced by her husband against her will, nor the husband by his wife. Nor is divorce possible 'by mutual consent'. Jesus Christ taught that when a husband and wife are joined in marriage, the two become *one flesh*. And He added, 'what God has joined together, let no man put asunder.' In other words, the marriage bond forged by God is so strong that no human being, nor even the married couple itself, has the power to break it. This was one of the reasons why God in the beginning fashioned the first woman from the side of the first man. It was as if He was saying to them, 'Remember that you, Eve, were formed from your husband, and that you, Adam, gave of your substance to make Eve; and know that you may not be separated as long as you both shall live.'

That's why the Church says that divorce is impossible for anyone, not just for Catholics. Whatever religion they profess, once a man and a woman have committed themselves to each other for life to the exclusion of all others, they become one in God's sight. So even if they later go to a court of law and get a certificate announcing that they are now divorced, the Church considers this of no real effect. In God's eyes, they are still married. In extreme cases, for example if the husband is very violent, they could separate, but neither can marry again whilst the first spouse is still living.

Is this unfair? It's surely the opposite that would be unfair. The possibility of divorce is unjust to the spouses themselves. How can they commit themselves to each other with all the loyalty needed to build a family if they know that they can have their marriage dissolved later on? God gives them the assurance that their marriage is unbreakable to support them in the hard task of raising children. Next, as you point out, divorce is also unfair on the children. It's very difficult for children to reverence their parents as God commands if their parents have ceased to reverence each other. Children revere their parents not so much as individuals, but as a unit, as *one thing*. If that one thing tears itself in two, what is the child supposed to do? Finally, divorce is unjust to society, since every divorce weakens the institution of marriage, and this institution needs to be strong for society to be in good health, as experience shows.

All the same, you say, shouldn't one allow divorce in 'hard cases'? One should have great compassion on those in unhappy marriages, but the problem is this. Once human beings take it upon themselves to make a breach in the wall with which God has surrounded marriage, this breach inexorably widens. The Catholic Church warned that this would happen, and history has surely proved her right. When divorce was first made legal in countries that had once been Catholic, it was only meant to be something exceptional – for example if the husband had become clinically insane. But when people saw that remarriage was possible on this ground, pressure began to mount to make it possible on some slightly less stringent ground, for example if the husband was violent. For human nature always tends to slip downwards from what is more demanding to what is less demanding unless it's held in place by firm principles. By an inevitable process, and one that hasn't really taken very long, we've reached our present state where divorces are granted to anyone who asks. Has that increased the happiness of the world?

So we say that the State has no power to end a marriage, whether of Christians or of others. When it says that it does, we say that it is simply mistaken.

There are only two exceptions that the Catholic Church allows to the principle that a duly contracted and consummated marriage can never be dissolved before death is as follows. Suppose you have a husband and a wife, neither of whom is baptized. One of them becomes a Christian. The other not only fails to become a Christian, but makes life intolerable for his or her spouse out of hatred for Christianity. In that case the Church says that the newly-baptized spouse is no longer bound by the marriage. The baptized spouse has become a new creation, and the unbaptized spouse has been unwilling to do even the minimum that could have been expected of him or her by the light of nature. So God in His mercy allows the Christian spouse to marry a fellow Christian, provided this is done by the Church's rites.

The second exception involves the circumstance where one of the parties in the marriage is unbaptized and the other is baptized. If either party wants to become Catholic, or wants to marry a Catholic, the first marriage can be dissolved, permitting the person to become Catholic or to marry a Catholic. These are special exceptions, which the Church has always allowed, and which end only non-sacramental, 'natural' marriages. We hold that these exceptions were revealed by the Holy Spirit in the days of the apostles, and since the death of the apostles the time of such revelations is ended.

What of the relation between husband and wife? They're called to the same eternal destiny. So our scriptures say that Christian spouses are 'co-heirs of the grace of life'. All the same, their roles in this life aren't identical. St Paul compares the husband and the wife to the head and body of a single person. The man is the 'head' of his wife, and of his family. He has the ultimate responsibility, before God, for the household. Therefore the wife should not do what she knows to be against her husband's will — unless, of course, he should ask her to do something sinful. Likewise, the husband must love and respect his wife, and show this by the consideration with which he treats her. She ought to be as dear to him as his own body. One of our modern popes has also said that if the father is the head of the household, the mother is its heart, and that as to him belongs the first place in governing, to her should belong the first place in loving.

By the way, you may know that marriage is one of the seven sacraments of the Church. A sacrament, remember, is a channel of grace coming from Christ to us. Whenever two people marry, their consent creates a bond between them which remains until one of them dies. And when two baptized people marry, God uses this bond to sanctify them. Just as He uses water in baptism to wash away original sin, so in this sacrament He uses the marriage bond to make the spouses holy. Provided they're faithful to His plan for marriage, their marriage itself will sanctify them.

Since Christian marriage is so holy a union, we compare it to the union between Christ and His Church. Christ is the bridegroom, and the Church is His bride. This shows us another reason why divorce is impossible. If a Christian marriage could be destroyed, it would no longer be an image of Christ and the Church. He'll never divorce His Church, because He's promised to be with her 'all days, even to the end of the age'.

That brings us to your last question, about polygamy. As you know, we hold that there's only one Church. So if a Christian were allowed to take more than one wife, his marriage would no longer manifest Christ's 'marriage' to the Church. But then it wouldn't be a sacrament: it wouldn't be holy enough. Before Christ came, polygamy was sometimes tolerated by God. A special dispensation was given to men like Abraham to take more than one wife, and so to beget many believing children who might make up for all the idolaters then living. Still, not everything recorded in the Old Testament is necessarily good. Solomon clearly had too many wives, and it led to his downfall. David didn't sin seriously by having so many wives; whether he did well by it, I don't know. But in the age of grace, in which we're living, those who marry are bound to one spouse only, 'until death do them part'.

With best wishes,
Christophorus

Letter Thirty-Two

ON FRUITFULNESS
IN MARRIAGE

Dear Ali,

You have another question to ask about Catholic beliefs on marriage. You say you've heard that the Church forbids Catholics from using contraception, and you wonder why that is. 'Is it simply so that Catholicism can grow faster than other religions? Or if that law is meant for everyone, wouldn't the world quickly become over-populated if everyone followed it?' And you say that while you agree that children are a blessing from God, you think that a married couple should also be able to decide when they've had enough children, especially if they're too poor to raise any more.

Let's go back to the beginning again, to what happened at Creation. According to the Book of Genesis, after God had created the man and the woman, He said to them, 'Be fruitful and multiply.' And to show that He wasn't just talking to that first couple, He added, 'Fill the earth'; which obviously Adam and Eve couldn't do by themselves. By these words, then, God must have been speaking to all married couples. He was inviting them to help complete His work of creation. You see, though God by Himself spread plants and trees and animals across the whole earth, and filled the waters with fish and other creatures, He didn't want to fill the world with human beings by Himself alone. He willed that human beings themselves should co-operate with Him to this goal.

See what a noble vocation God has given to married people. He invites them to do something which the angels themselves can't do; to complete His creation. The angels help to govern the world, they watch over the elements and all the species of plant and animal that God has made, but they don't *add* anything to the creation. A husband and wife, on the other hand, have power to bring an entirely new being into creation. They can cause a new person to exist, a child endowed with an immortal soul (it's true that God Himself creates the soul directly, since it's a spirit, but He waits for the parents' co-operation before He does). By their married love, the couple can bring into existence something of more value than the sun and all the stars: a new human being.

Is this all? No. Their children are intended by God to be not only inhabitants of the earth, but also citizens of heaven. He wants married couples to have children whom He may adopt as His own sons and daughters. That's why He grants to parents sacred rights that no earthly power may infringe, to raise their children in true religion, and so reach heaven at the end of their lives. Think what happiness fathers or mothers must have after death when they see that not only have they saved their own souls, but also that their children have become 'equal to the angels'. By their generosity on earth, parents can help God to fill up the heavenly city. They can increase the glory that God will receive for all eternity. Finally, they can bring nearer the moment when the number of the saints will be complete; and when that happens, according to our faith, God's Kingdom will be revealed in all its glory, and the devil will be vanquished.

Reflect on this for a while, and then think what contraception is. It's the opposite of all that. It summons up the power of procreation and then turns it away from these goals for which God created it. It prevents new persons, endowed with immortal souls, from entering the world. It denies the couple the happiness of becoming the parents of future saints. It slows down the growth of God's Kingdom, and refuses to increase the glory that God will receive for eternity. It delays the triumph of His Kingdom, and prolongs the time during which the fallen spirits will have power over men. That's why God's holy law has forbidden it. The Church didn't forbid it on her own initiative. She has simply made known to us God's will.

In other words, my friend, the Church considers that children are a gift from God in a unique way. Everything that exists is held in being by God, and so it's His gift to us. But when a child is conceived, God sends something new into the world: a new immortal soul. And a married couple can't be in harmony with God if they're blocking the doorway, so to speak, by which souls enter creation.

Is this an easy teaching for married couples? No, for many of them it isn't, especially in the world today. But then Christ didn't say that it would be easy to believe in Him, but rather that it would make us blessed: blessed by anticipation here, blessed in full reality hereafter. And when married couples obey God's will in this matter, it's an important part of their way to final blessedness. Remember what I said last time, that when Christians marry, their very marriage is a sacrament. Their marriage itself sanctifies them when they live according to God's law. God doesn't expect married people to spend many hours in church every day, or to fast a lot, or to give a great deal of time to reading the sacred scriptures and the writings of the saints. He knows they have other things to do. But He does want them to become holy, and holiness must always mean sacrifice. As St Luke puts it, 'through many tribulations we must come to the kingdom of God.'

If a husband and wife are genuinely afraid that they won't be able to feed or clothe another child, then they can abstain from their marital relations for a time. They're not obliged, after all, to have all the children which it's physically possible to have. Yet I think that if they're generous, they'll desire to extend their family and God's as much as they can, somewhat as a zealous priest would want to bring as many souls as possible to Christ.

What I'm saying is a long way from the received wisdom of our age, I know. But then St Paul says, 'the wisdom of this world is foolishness with God.' Our modern Western nations have relied on the wisdom of the world and too late they're now regretting their lack of children. They've made life hard for those who desired to have children, and for women who might have devoted themselves to motherhood. If only they'd listened to Christ's Church! They mightn't now be in danger of collapsing.

But what of your other objection, that if all married couples followed what the Church says, then the world would soon have more people than it could support? No one knows how many people our world can support. There are still vast tracts of land which are hardly inhabited. Some of these tracts of land are barren at the moment, it's true; but if all human beings were living according to the Gospel of Christ, surely some of the money now spent on terrible weapons of warfare, or on journeys into space, would be spent instead on irrigating deserts or improving farming in poor lands.

But more importantly, if we believe the words of Jesus Christ, we know that this world where people marry and are given in marriage is not going to continue forever. He's promised that He'll return and put an end to history. If we believe that, it doesn't take much more faith to believe that He also knows when to return, and that He won't return too late! God wouldn't allow mankind to come to disaster by following His will.

With best wishes,
Christophorus

Letter Thirty-Three

ON FOLLOWING CHRIST

Dear Ali,

You say that you've no more questions, at least for now, about the Catholic faith itself. You see how it fits together, and why we believe it. But you do want to ask a few last questions, all the same. 'Can anyone who's born outside Christianity ever really fit into the Church? Wouldn't he always be looked upon as an outsider?' And a little later you write, 'Family ties are so important, as you said in the letter about divorce, that perhaps God doesn't intend people to risk cutting themselves off from their family by changing religion. I could believe that Catholicism is the true religion, but can God really want someone to join it at the cost of losing his friends and becoming estranged from his family? Wouldn't He be content for someone to worship Him and lead a good life in this world? After all, you said that some may go to heaven even without having been baptized with water. Perhaps it's only in heaven that all believers will be of one religion.'

I understand why someone might reason in that way, and I'd sympathize with anyone in the position you describe. But in answer to your first question, yes, someone who is born and brought up outside the

Catholic Church can really find his home within it. In fact, *everyone* is born outside the Church. Christianity isn't a religion like Judaism, which a person belongs to because his parents did. We're all born with original sin; we only enter the Church when we're baptized.

But more than that, many people who've grown up outside the Church and even been hostile to her have entered the Church as adults and found their home within her. Some of them were even persecutors of the Church before they believed. Take St Paul, for instance. He tells us that he was educated to be very zealous for all the traditions of his people, the Jews. He was very proud of belonging to the chosen people, with its Law that set it apart from all other peoples on earth. So he was very hostile to the Church when he first met it, because he could see that it would be incompatible with the Judaism he knew. So he started doing all he could to destroy the Church, and to have her members chained up or killed. You know the rest of the story: he met the risen Christ on the way to Damascus, he believed and he was baptized. He spent the rest of his life spreading the Gospel among the pagans. Not only did St Paul 'find a place' within the Church, but he and St Peter are reckoned as the two greatest apostles of all.

It's the same in every generation. People are brought up outside the Church and perhaps have many prejudices against it, but God's grace reaches them and changes their heart. They discover that Christ is the Son of God, and they want to live by His teaching. Sometimes, on entering the Church, they show a zeal that puts 'cradle Catholics' to shame. Of course it takes them a little while to become used to the idea of being Catholic, but that soon passes, and then they begin to wonder how they could have lived outside the Church for so long. After all, the Catholic Church *is* our home, intended by God for all mankind – so why should we doubt that we can find our home within her?

But in the end, it's not our feelings that matter, but simply the truth. If we believe that Christ's teachings are true, we've a duty to follow them, come what may. After all, even the pagan philosopher knew that 'we must follow the argument wherever it leads'. If that's true when the argument concerns only human ideas, how much more when it concerns the road to salvation!

You ask if God wants people to become Christians even at the cost of friendships and family ties. God is good, so He always wants what is good. It's good for us to know that Christ is His Son and that the Church unites us to Christ. God can't want us to miss the salvation that comes to us from Christ and the Church. Of course, God values family affection. He placed it in our hearts in the first place. But family affection isn't the greatest of goods; if we made it so, we'd stop being good. Nothing can be more important than God and His will.

Yes, it's true I said in an earlier letter that some may be saved even though they aren't received in a public way into the Catholic Church. But this could only apply to those who are overtaken by death before they've fully understood their duties or before they can accomplish them. It can't apply to those who know that God wants them to belong to Christ, but who turn their eyes away from His will.

Jesus told us that we must be ready to forego everything else, if necessary, to gain eternal life. He once said,

'Whoever would save his life, shall lose it; and whoever shall lose his life for my sake and the gospel, he shall save it.' Or again, 'He that loves father or mother more than me, is not worthy of me; and he that loves son or daughter more than me is not worthy of me.'

Yet the corollary is that if we do prefer God and His truth to everything else, nothing can ever really harm us. God will be in our soul, and no created power can touch the soul. That's why our Lord said, 'Do not fear those who kill the body and after that have no more that they can do.' Persecutors can harm a man's body or separate him from his family and friends; but they can't take God away from him, nor can they keep him away from heaven.

If we prefer truth above all else then God will take us to heaven at the end of our lives. He will give us a place among His children, equal to the angels. Jesus Christ once declared: 'Everyone that shall confess me before men, I also will confess before my Father who is in heaven'; and 'He who endures to the end, he shall be saved.'

Above all, pray much. The devil tempts everyone, and it's by prayer that we overcome him. So don't listen to him if he tries to tell you what you might lose by becoming a Christian. Instead, keep your mind fixed on what God has promised to those who love and serve Him: eternal happiness in His kingdom. You can pray the prayer that St Peter spoke when he tried to walk like Christ on the waters and began to sink beneath the waves: 'Lord, save me or I perish!' Or you could pray this ancient prayer, 'Lord Jesus Christ, Son of the living God, have mercy on me a sinner.' Pray to the Blessed Virgin, as well, Mary the Mother of Christ. I know that you were taught to respect her when you were growing up. But she's a much more powerful person than you realize yet. Ask her for her help, and she won't fail you. You could use the same words that the angel used when he was announcing the Incarnation, 'Hail, full of grace, the Lord is with thee'.

That's all I have to say. But know that I'll be praying for you, and what's much more, the whole Church will be praying for you wherever the holy mysteries are offered. 'He who has the Son, has life. . . . If the Son shall make you free, you shall be free indeed.'

With best wishes,

Christophorus

Lightning Source UK Ltd.
Milton Keynes UK
UKOW03f0845060514

231179UK00001B/32/P